Fred Brown moved from darkest city to deepest country a few years ago and now writes from his cottage in South-East Kent.

By the same author

Happy

FRED BROWN

The Grass is Greener

GRAFTON BOOKS

A Division of the Collins Publishing Group

LONDON GLASGOW
TORONTO SYDNEY AUCKLAND

Grafton Books
A Division of the Collins Publishing Group
8 Grafton Street, London W1X 3LA

Published by Grafton Books 1988

ISBN 0-586-07220-9

Printed and bound in Great Britain by
Collins, Glasgow

Set in Times

To celebrate
Corrie
Sammy
Suzie and
Daisy

Author's Note

The village of this book epitomizes our experiences since my wife and I moved to an isolated cottage in Kent after a quarter of a century of living and working in London.

For easier presentation of some of the material, I have occasionally changed the chronology and not hesitated to treat two or three similar personalities and events as one.

Contents

1

The bird in the chimney – and removing it the country way

Friday Night

A whole weekend in our new country setting stretched before us. Time to tackle a few more odd jobs – repair the leaking roof of the decrepit barn we were allowed to use (possible home, we fantasized with serious intent, for the goats we planned), clear the ditch behind the cottage, and return to our assault on the less than co-operative cesspit.

The following morning, responding to the dawn chorus, I sprang out of bed, hummed a welcome to the day as I made coffee, and sipped it with my wife as periodically we gazed through the window at the paradise all around us.

At first we didn't pay much attention to the noise coming from the chimney in the lounge, doubtless the stronger than usual draughts exploring our excess of nooks and crannies in that region. In any case, we were in the kitchen, having breakfast with everything conveniently to hand, including our lovely Aga. And the cottage was a notorious creaker and groaner, rarely entirely silent as a result, I suppose, of its solid foundations and oak beams withstanding the building's exposure to the elements.

Even so, this noise from the lounge finally demanded investigation. I looked up the chimney. Nothing. Yet there it was again, a frantic fluttering of wings followed by falling soot.

I continued to peer up the chimney, once more seeing

nothing, but as my eyes adjusted to the semi-darkness I spotted a bird, almost the size of a pigeon, on a ledge. Spasmodically it beat its wings, unable to go up, too frightened, presumably, to come down. Meanwhile the trickle of soot stretched my wife's benevolence.

'Poor thing.' Her concern for the bird was predominant. 'What shall we do?'

'What *can* we do?' I asked; and throughout the rest of the morning our impotence was confirmed. We put food in the hearth. The bird ignored it. We banged a tin lid. The bird's only response was more futile fluttering.

I changed into old clothes, and tried to reach the bird. The result was predictable – cascading soot, wings fluttering madly, and a ready made-up applicant for the George Mitchell choir.

We tried, God knows we tried, but all our efforts were of no avail. By lunch time I was knackered; soot was pouring out of my ears, my nose, and into my eyes, mouth, pockets and shoes. Trying to be philosophical about the situation, we had a snack, and – a weekend indulgence of mine – I took myself off to the woods half way between our village and the next, one of my very favourite places, guarantee of absolute aloneness.

Each time I went there I was forcibly reminded of Thomas Hardy's opening to *Under the Greenwood Tree*, a book I'd discovered, or rather read, only after coming here:

To dwellers in a wood, almost every species of tree has its voice as well as its feature. At the passing of the breeze, the fir-trees sob and moan no less distinctly than they rock; the holly whistles as it battles with itself; the ash hisses amid its quivering; the beech rustles while its flat boughs rise and fall. And winter, which modifies the notes of such trees as they shed their leaves, does not destroy its individuality.

On this occasion I was alone, or so I thought, confirming yet again the music of the trees, when the playful welcome from a black Labrador alerted me to the presence of another human. He looked as surprised as I felt. We muttered greetings, mentioned the weather, and almost certainly would have continued our separate ways, ships, as they say, passing in the night, but his dog was remarkably friendly, rushing from one to the other, making conversation inevitable.

He told me he'd just sighted a weasel chasing a wood mouse; the two had disappeared into the undergrowth, and after a flurry the mouse had triumphantly emerged to make good its escape, not a sign of paralysis through fear.

We introduced ourselves! He said he'd been a woodman all his life, like his father, and grandfather, the three of them sharing a love affair with trees.

'Smell this!' he commanded, picking up a piece of chestnut. 'The tang! Isn't it beautiful!'

I could only marvel at the capacity of this bit of old firewood to get him going. Nothing demonstrative, you understand, never more than a word or two. But his reticence was all the more convincing. I wanted to know further about how and why he felt so deeply about trees.

As we walked to the turning he told me he worked in the woods six days a week, first light to mid-afternoon, usually seeing no one, his only company his faithful dog.

'Never lonely?' I asked almost facetiously.

His reaction astonished me, suggesting I'd put my finger on a guilty secret. The quietness of the woods, he confessed, sometimes nearly drove him crazy. It was, he tried to explain, as though the endless silence created a vacuum in his mind, a vacuum into which rushed terrifying thoughts – mocking, accusing, threatening. The only way he could cope was to do his work against a background of

13

Radio One, the sort of music neither he nor his wife could stand at home.

'Strange, isn't it?' he smiled.

'Have you ever thought about changing your job?' I must have sounded profoundly obvious.

His gentle eyes filled with steel. 'I couldn't stand a factory,' he said, 'penned up for hours on end. No, this is the job for me. I love it. And working anywhere else wouldn't make any difference to my mind. I've always been like it, well, since I was sixteen or so.'

We reached the turning, and I made to follow a path to the right, my way home. He laughed. 'You going to the hermit's place, then?' he asked.

My eyes surely filled with question marks. I didn't realize anyone lived within miles.

'Haven't you heard about the hermit!' The woodman was now enjoying himself.

I admitted my ignorance, but before he had time to say anything a thrush, appearing to ignore us altogether, perched itself on a nearby hornbeam and simply galvanized our attention with its song. The woodman was doubtless accustomed to such symphonies, but his enchantment was clearly no less than mine.

'Noisy little bugger,' he summed up affectionately as the bird finally flew away.

Inevitably in the circumstances my mind did a bit of flying too, back to the bird in our chimney, and I mentioned the dilemma. 'I suppose it will die,' I concluded, 'we've tried everything to get it out.'

He looked at me with the kind of indulgence or patronage countrymen reserve, I've discovered, for conversations with city dwellers and ex-townees alike. Slowly his face creased into a smile, rather like a man in an argument who knows he's about to prove his superiority.

'Bird in your chimney!' He smacked his lips.

I found myself responding to his gaiety, for he actually made the situation sound amusing, something of a joke, the very opposite in truth of my feelings. Only slowly did the alien thought emerge that he wasn't laughing at the bird's plight but at my ineptitude.

'I can tell you what to do,' he said; and I listened to what he assured me was an old country method of dislodging birds from chimneys. It sounded altogether too simple, not to say far-fetched, and I imagine my eyes revealed my scepticism.

'Never fails,' he reiterated, 'not in my experience, and I've done it often.' By way of illustration of the method's infallibility, he told me the last time he used it was to remove a bird from the chimney of an old-age pensioner living alone. 'Near frightened her to death,' he said, 'bloody magpie it was; didn't give the old lady a moment's peace with its chattering and squawking. Soon had it out!'

By now he was moving along the path deeper into the wood, his dog no longer rushing between us but dutifully to heel. 'Let me know how you get on,' he called. 'I'm usually in the woods somewhere.'

I've never seen him again, but I shan't forget his method of getting a bird out of a chimney in a hurry. Neither will my wife!

'Is it worth a try?' I said to her on reaching home.

'We've nothing to lose,' she couldn't wait to start, unmindful as I was of the implications of what we were about to attempt.

'Right!' I finished the briefing strictly in accordance with the woodman's instructions. 'Let's see what happens.'

'Is that *all*!' She sounded incredulous. 'I mean, what if anything goes wrong!'

'Nothing can go wrong.' I handed her the torch, and spread the *Guardian* over the mouth of the chimney. Admittedly this proved to be less straightforward than I'd anticipated, but eventually it was, like the pair of us, firmly in place.

My wife shone the torch through the paper up the chimney. The response was ear-splitting silence. If the bird was still alive it had obviously never heard of this means of rescue. Resolutely I continued to support the paper, treating with contempt the first intimations of doubt flitting through my mind.

'This is silly.' My wife typically understated the case.

We crouched there, she shining the torch, I holding the paper, for no more than a minute that nevertheless seemed an age. The trickle of soot continued spasmodically. We thought we heard fluttering. Then – in a trice – the bird hit the paper, proceeded straight through, and, despite my frantic grabs, was flying round the lounge squawking like crazy. Meanwhile the sprinkling from the chimney developed into an avalanche and rose like a mushroom cloud. Not that I noticed at the time.

I chased the bird from the lounge to the kitchen to the bathroom back to the kitchen into the lounge and BANG! – it hit the window with a thud and dropped to the carpet as dead.

My wife groaned. I stopped in my tracks, gazed in horror at the poor creature, and actually stepped back, suddenly awestruck or afraid to pick it up. Strange. Whatever the explanation, I shouldn't have hesitated to get my hands on it!

The corpse opened first one eye, then the other, and in no time the pair of us were careering from the lounge to

16

the kitchen to the bathroom back to the kitchen and into the lounge. BANG!

This time I did pick it up. So tenderly. And immediately dropped it as it dug its giant beak into my hand. But this time it didn't fall to the carpet. Bloody bird. Off it went again from the lounge to the kitchen . . .

Now, however, there was one almighty difference as I gave chase. My wife opened the window. It flew out apparently none the worse for our misadventure, leaving us gasping, breathing soot, and triumphant; fairly triumphant. True, we didn't entirely see eye to eye about the effectiveness of this reputedly traditional country method of retrieving birds from chimneys; and cleaning up operations did further delay my attempts to repair the leaking barn. But beyond peradventure we had saved the bird – a jackdaw, our birdbook confirmed – from certain death, not to mention our chimney from the blockage of a corpse. Who cared about a speck or two of soot!

Within no more than a couple of hours the cottage was shining with carbolic freshness, a lingering smell of charcoal the only suggestion of the recent chaos. Even the kettle on the Aga was singing louder than usual.

We made tea, sank our weary limbs, and oozed contentment. What a life! And re-living the episode we nearly choked with laughter.

'There's only one thing that disappoints me,' I tried to sound as serious as I felt, 'the woodman didn't finish his story about the hermit.'

'The hermit?'

'According to the woodman,' I repeated, 'there's a hermit's place in the woods.'

'Here,' she reached out her hand, 'let me pour you another cup of tea.'

2

The donkey cottager

I had always been happiest with pavements beneath my feet. To be away from London, home for twenty-five years, even for holidays, was something of a trial, only resolved by my return to the beloved pollution and noise.

Then, out of the blue – for family reasons I could neither remotely anticipate nor at first quite believe – my wife and I found ourselves contemplating a move to the country.

A dream cottage! Deep in the Garden of England.

Everybody told us how fortunate we were, and of course we believed them. Unreservedly. True, our new situation was going to involve a change of job for us both – for me a daily round journey of eighty miles, Monday to Friday – but think, we reassured each other, of the weekends and long summer evenings – peace and quiet, chance for our souls to catch up with our bodies, time to stand and stare . . . we indulged every cliché imaginable.

The good life was just around the corner!

From the start we tended to under-estimate the mud, a common failing, I believe, of ex-city starry-eyed romantics. Indisputably, let there be no misunderstanding, the countryside is charming – idyllic! – but the need to change into wellies before trudging from car to your own back door a field away can be less than endearing. Actually, to be absolutely honest, at least half the trouble was our own impatience.

All right, so the cottage wasn't quite ready; the

plumber, the painter, and proverbial candlestick-maker were still leaping all over the place; the carpet wasn't down, some of the flooring was so newly laid a haze of concrete dust rose every time anybody walked from kitchen to lounge.

Not that this mattered. Even the final part of our approach to the cottage, an almost mile long dirt road, deeply pitted, parts of it seemingly permanently water-logged, didn't remotely deter us. Come what may, we were going to be in by Christmas, only weeks away, and nothing, least of all our well exercised city caution, was going to stop us.

There was logic in this madness, too. With the family getting together anyway for our customary Christmas Eve festivities, wouldn't it be great, the children and their partners shared our excitement, to gather at the cottage!

Fantastic.

Like us, they couldn't wait to see us installed. So as the craftsmen with their tools moved out, we moved in, a little before two o'clock on Christmas Eve itself. By the time the preparation of the celebratory meal was well underway the haze from the floor compelled us to call to each other to stay in touch.

What fun!

Naturally we'd warned everybody that wellies were indispensable. And it didn't seem to matter when one of the early arrivals appeared to derive disproportionate pleasure from falling flat on his face in the mud. Even his mother, city girl if ever there was one, shared the merriment as this liveliest grandchild was wrung out and washed down, remarkable proof of Christmas goodwill.

We heard the final car cross the third cattle grid, and watched from the kitchen window as the headlights picked out first the pond, then the ancient farmhouse, and finally focused on the gate leading to the field and the cottage.

It was, we gathered, at this moment of triumph – they'd found the place after all! – that the wife of the driver groaned.

The wellies!

Her husband had forgotten to put the wellies in the car!

They both viewed the quagmire beyond the gate, she utterly convinced that her high-heeled shoes were hardly suitable for country walking. As for the two children's delicate footwear, never mind her husband's near dance pumps . . .

Gently, without malice aforethought, she appealed to his gallantry. Would he care to make his way to the cottage to borrow the necessary wellies? Typically he didn't hesitate. Casting his eyes over the nature of the barrier between himself and his destination, he decided this was time for a Sir Walter Raleigh gesture, not of course with a cloak but his car, surely powerful enough to plough through the mud to the Christmas lights beckoning.

His perspicacious wife urged caution.

The engine roared.

I grabbed a lantern and ran.

Alas, by the time I arrived, the marooned quartet had already abandoned 'ship' and – with a conspicuous absence of festive cheer – were up to their knees in mud.

Happy Christmas!

And in the end so it proved. Sheer magic. I can't help but wonder, though, what would have happened without the kindly farmer's rescuing tractor? Pity, too, about those fashionable shoes. They never did recover.

City people who move to the country and remain city people at heart find their new surroundings intolerable. A

20

veritable nightmare. Some of our friends paying an early visit were unnerved by the pitch blackness of the night, unknown with city lighting, and by what can perhaps be best described as the silence beneath silence – that absolute stillness paradoxically accentuated and often made eerie by creaking tree or hooting owl in the small hours before dawn.

Prior to coming here I used to think there were few things more plaintive – or soothing! – than the moo of a cow; gentle appeal of hope, evocative of country peace. Then I heard one bulling.

There's a herd of Friesians behind our cottage. Most of the time we hardly know they're there, but occasionally one comes into season, broadcasting like a foghorn its urgent necessity in a bull-less world.

At one time a bull roamed freely with the herd, sniffing out partners ready to receive him, and earning his not inexpensive keep by appropriately rising to the occasion. These days, as I quickly discovered, bulling is answered by a representative from the milk board! And that wasn't the only surprise.

A car pulled into the farmyard, and out stepped a beautiful young woman. She followed the farmer into his cowshed, fiddled in her black bag for the semen of his favoured breed, and eventually – with the unhurried confidence of a hardened practitioner – pushed her hand up the cow's backside.

'That should do the trick,' she said. 'If it doesn't take, give us a ring; won't cost you extra.' She laughed reassuringly. And cleaning up at the farm tap, she talked shop with a cultured accent, as unlike the traditional country dweller as it's possible to imagine.

Never mind the convenience of this new arrangement, the farmer prefers it because it's far cheaper than keeping a bull of his own. What, however, the cow, not to mention the bull, thinks of it all is something else.

I imagine the cow shared our astonishment at the unnaturalness of nature! With eyes and ears unattuned to our new surroundings, my wife and I inwardly stood on tiptoe, often could barely believe the evidence of our own eyes, looked and listened again to confirm we weren't being deceived, and whooped like children.

No wonder one of our first preoccupations, finally almost an obsession, was to find a name for the cottage. Significantly we'd never felt like this about any of our city abodes – a *number* had been both adequate and appropriate – but now we wanted a *name*, one that bespoke not only our lovely surroundings but equally the sense of fun and wonderment we increasingly experienced; experienced, incidentally, often beyond the comprehension of some of our new neighbours, born and bred in the country. They were, I suspect, in their friendly way, a little amused at our excitement, and waited for us to settle down.

Happily one of them inadvertently brought home to me the crucial importance of finding the right name for the cottage. Rounding a bend on one of my early walks of exploration, I stopped in my tracks and gawped.

A young woman, decidedly attractive, being exercised by her dog! And what a dog – almost as tall as herself, indisputably stronger, and fiercely provoked. Fiercely? A couple of canine pipsqueaks indulging their harmless yapping behind the sturdy fence of a house set well back in its own grounds. I'd already suffered their noisy bravado myself, and knew they couldn't frighten a dead rabbit between them.

Yes, but how does a shire horse pretending to be a dog perceive the difference between harmless yapping and fighting talk? It struggled furiously, determined to teach these upstarts a lesson. The louder they yapped the more it fought to get at them, hindered by the woman, airborne and horizontal on the lead, no less than the unyielding fence. She held on for dear life.

Then she spotted me!

I was, needless to say, genuinely lost in admiration of her do-or-die spirit, wanting nothing more than to help this damsel in distress. Uncertain only how. She blushed. I mean the colour of a lobster, from ear to ear. Self-evidently, to cope with her four-legged juggernaut was one thing, to have someone – barely a villager, to boot – witness the unequal contest was insufferable.

My belated offer of gallantry was declined. Taking the hint, I hurried past staring ostentatiously in the other direction.

Next day, to her obvious consternation, I met her again, this time wrestling not with her dog, prowling protectively in the garden, but a lawn mower no less defiant. My intention was, of course, to speed past – until I noticed, couldn't avoid noticing, the name of the house, beautifully inscribed in the brickwork of a pillar supporting the garden gate. An intriguing name.

I glanced in her direction.

She smiled.

I called good morning.

She reciprocated.

So – submitting to a temerity somehow unthinkable in the city – I wondered aloud about the name.

Followed by the dog she strolled over. When the house was being built, she and her husband, impatient to move into their first marital home, kept asking the builder when he expected to finish – the foundations, walls, roof, lounge, bedrooms, and so on, section by section. His reply never varied.

Roundabout Friday.

She paused. 'We decided,' her embarrassment deepened by the second, 'we decided to call the house Roundabout Friday.'

She expected me, I think, to laugh, as though the name was too silly for words. In fact, I responded enthusiastically, recognizing that such a name evoked all the hopes and dreams associated with the building of the house.

'That's the sort of name we want,' I said to my wife on reaching home, 'something personal, intimate, a name that gathers to itself a whole range of on-going endearments known only to those in the inner circle.'

Yet still the name remained on the tip of our tongues. We toyed with numerous near misses, sought suggestions from family and friends, settled for Ewe Smile, changed our minds within hours, and purred with profound contentment as eventually the name simply chose itself.

You see, our cottage is hidden by hedgerows and trees, virtually unfindable from spring until the leaves fall. As though this isn't enough lots of people in the village appear not to realize the solitary cottage is here at all. A few of the really old-timers vaguely remember a farm labourer's cottage in our general direction, but precisely *where*, even supposing their memory isn't playing them tricks, they've little idea.

Some of our visitors, going round in circles trying to find us, have met disbelief in the village on mentioning our address. One old man, his roots here for generations, insisted no such place existed in these parts.

One urbanite friend, within five minutes of arriving, told us our isolation gave her the creeps. Another facetiously suggested we call the place End of the World or

Beyond the Beyond, neither intended as a commendation, I'm sure.

Whichever way you looked at it, we were off the beaten track, reachable most easily by helicopter. So the name that chose us seemed just about perfect.

Hide 'n' Seek!

Hide 'n' Seek cottage, reminiscent of the magic of childhood, our feelings more and more. We also discovered that once a home is lovingly named it somehow assumes an entirely new relationship with the people living under its roof. We were bound to be starry-eyed. Whatever lay ahead, disillusionment or not, romanticism about living in the country took over. Henceforth, life for us would consist of surely the sweetest and most welcome alarm clock in the world, the dawn chorus; butterflies swarming the buddleia within view of the lounge window; lambs gambolling just beyond the garden gate; our own cultivated vegetables and flowers; hens foraging round the back door; and – all in good time – perhaps a couple of goats for milk and home-made cheese. With a name like Hide 'n' Seek cottage anything was possible.

To be fair, it didn't take our city sophistication long to sus out that milk didn't really come from bottles, lambs weren't born hygienically packaged at supermarkets, and squirrels didn't wear woolly hats. But this apart, we knew as much about living in the country as skunks about the manufacture of perfume.

One of our first problems was to decide what to do with a triangle of land grandiosely called 'the paddock' opposite the cottage. Hardly big enough to swing a cat, even a small cat, it was further reduced by over-grown hedges and trees, about as much like a paddock as a horse box, and liable to turn any attempt to walk through it into an obstacle race. Only as we began to piece together bits of local history did the title – paddock! – make any sense at all.

Actually, we were fortunate in that one of our earliest local visitors was a retired shepherd whose forebears, he claimed, were among the first patrons of the ancient village pub. Long, long ago, he explained, when our cottage was much less grand than now, it was bought by an outsider – a man from the next village – whose wife made no secret that the love of her life was a pet donkey.

She proved it, the old shepherd chuckled, by stabling the creature on the ground floor of the cottage while she and her husband lived upstairs. 'Must have been a hell of a job,' he interpreted the question mark in my eyes, 'getting the silly bugger through the front door.'

We laughed together, I perhaps excessively, convinced the old man was pulling the leg of this self-confessed country greenhorn. 'It's God's truth, I tell you,' he accepted my scepticism as a personal affront, 'the donkey lived downstairs. Ask anybody round here,' he concluded.

My eyes again measured that door, and I tried to imagine a donkey passing in and out. 'Didn't they,' my innocence asked, 'have a problem with, well, hygiene?'

'You mean shit!' He proudly paraded the countryman's badge for plain speaking. 'Donkeys shit clean. Like horses. Have you ever seen a horse or donkey with a dirty arse?' He warmed to his theme.

I admitted I hadn't.

'There you are, then.' He sounded triumphant. 'You won't get cleaner shit than from horses and donkeys. Nice and dry, you see,' my enlightenment continued, 'no need to wipe their backsides. All the roughage they eat!'

He cast this final pearl of information with a deadpan face, a face suddenly burdened, as though, in the middle

26

of a joke, the teller remembered he'd left the bath running. 'I've been a shepherd all my life,' he announced; 'Sheep are dirty buggers. Shit all over themselves.'

He paused, for a moment lost in thought. 'I'd like as many pound notes or these new fangled coins as I've dagged sheep's arses. You know,' he saw the need to explain, 'trimmed the soiled wool round their backsides; specially before lambing,' he added. 'Sheep can't keep 'emselves clean. Not like horses and donkeys.'

Once more I glanced at the cottage and the resplendent freshly painted door, still not entirely convinced the old shepherd wasn't taking an ex-townee – not universally popular in the country, I'd been warned – for a ride. I mean, the cottage *now* was so comfortable, mod cons, the lot, it took a bit of believing that a donkey was once part of a family living there.

'Was it permitted to turn part of a cottage into a stable?' I smiled. 'Didn't people need planning permission or something?'

The old shepherd looked amused; benign. 'In them days,' he said, 'folk weren't so particular. You could do what you liked with your own property. Not like today! There's bound to be some bloody form or other to fill in. And those government officials and their regulations!' he muttered.

'So the donkey explains why the bit of land opposite was called the paddock?' I pushed my enquiry.

'That's about it,' he said, 'can't think of any other reason.'

Again he paused, searching my face, his gentle eyes dancing with merriment. 'Have you heard the other bit of folklore associated with the paddock?' he asked.

According to village gossip, he began, this triangle of land was a bone of contention for years. Who owned it?

27

The farmer working the adjacent land or the man in the big house whose estate incorporated the cottage? Neither would budge. Each accused the other of dishonesty. At least dishonesty!

The village was divided right down the middle. The farmer's labourers and their families supported the farmer. The estate workers, knowing which side their bread was buttered, supported their lord and master. What else could the poor buggers do? The shepherd chortled.

A tiny doubt was already nagging at the back of my mind. How come two men with plenty of land thought it worth while to squabble over such an inconsequential patch as the paddock?

The old shepherd sounded like a schoolmaster addressing a backward pupil as he spat out that it was the *principle* of the thing. And their pride, I shouldn't wonder, he added. By all accounts, he continued, the estate owner was a bit of a rebel; openly supported the French revolution which didn't go down at all well in our village!

He waited for this political observation to register, perhaps wondering whether elaboration was necessary, but presumably assured it wasn't he turned and pointed to the woods about half-a-mile away as the crow flies. Have you, he asked, come across the tomb in the middle of the field by the woods? I indicated no. Well, that's where the estate owner's wife and two children are buried.

The parson wouldn't have 'em in the village church-yard. He said the estate owner himself and anybody contaminated by his dangerous ideas weren't fit to rest in consecrated ground. So the wife and children lie in yon field; beautiful spot, the old sheepman murmured, adding he wouldn't mind such a place when his time came.

What happened when the estate owner died? Did the parson relent?

Nobody knows. Nobody round here, the shepherd replied. He ain't with his wife and nippers in the vault, that's for sure. Just the three of 'em up there. Don't suppose it'll keep 'em out of heaven, he laughed. Some folk say the estate owner sold up and left the district, but it's only hearsay. We don't know what happened.

And what about the paddock? Did they ever sort out who owned it? I reminded him of his unfinished tale. They fought over it, he said, a proper prize fight, bare knuckled, like they did in them days, till one of 'em was beat. No idea who won. Silly buggers. All that fuss about nothing. Reckon the man not in the tomb was the winner, the old shepherd indulged his winsome sense of humour.

On hearing the story my wife was uncharitable enough to suspect I *had* been taken for a ride – paddock, donkey, vault, fight-to-a-finish, the lot. But then another villager of acknowledged unimpeachable integrity came up with the same story about the bare-knuckled set-to for the paddock. The main difference was he didn't identify the estate owner with the vault builder, convinced that the latter, whatever his revolutionary ideas, was too much a member of the aristocracy to engage in common fisticuffs!

Anyhow, I still couldn't really understand how anyone could get so heated about our so-called paddock. Even an erstwhile donkey neighbour must have found it rather cramped, not to mention a bit sparse on pasture, something we ourselves were able to confirm after acquiring a sheep (the infamous Baa-Baa) and her lamb; but this misadventure belongs to a later part of the story.

Of more immediate concern was what actually to do with the paddock? Here we were with a wilderness, no matter how small, stuck outside our front door. Drastic action, a massive cleaning up operation, was required.

Ah, yes, but the more we thought about it, allowed all the back-breaking implications to appeal to our lingering city sentiments, the more convinced we became that the sensible, not to say responsible, thing to do was to leave well alone. In the name of ecology, naturally!

'What about the hedge?' my wife responded.

'The hedge?' I appealed.

'That's right, the hedge,' she sucked on the word. 'We can't leave it as it is.'

I gazed upon it with new affection, only slowly realizing she wasn't referring to the paddock's hedge, but the eyesore in our front garden. Correction; our *potential* front garden. It was, beyond argument, a tatty hedge whose innumerable briars would sometimes, I swear, leap out to grab unsuspecting passers-by.

Nevertheless the occasional bird alighted upon it, and by the look of things one had once almost nested in it. I liked it. In any case, we were landed with it, briars, gaping holes, emaciated innards, the lot. My gentle wife disagreed. It was, she said, a shambles, a deterrent to spring, a barrier to the flower garden upon which her heart was set.

We hesitated for weeks, even argued, my one concern to save her from the vandalism I knew she'd regret. What clinched the matter was her reminder that after all we had decided for strictly ecological reasons to leave the paddock as a wilderness. Surely after such sacrifice we were entitled to remove this apology for a hedge?

The conservationist in me made one final appeal. True, the hedge was senile, even, to be really unkind, moribund; but – as the good book or somebody said – while there's life there's hope!

The agony of this indecision was resolved by my wife's

single-mindedness. Like a soldier sloping arms she advanced with fork and spade, handed me the latter, and led the charge. Within minutes we, never mind the hedge, were undone. In truth, only people who have never wrestled with the roots of briars and brambles could imagine for a moment that manual digging was remotely the answer.

Perhaps after all the hedge didn't look too bad!

Then my wife remembered Farmer Greendale.

Now Farmer Greendale, apart from running his own arable and sheep farm, is a contract farmer – hires out his men and machines to people who find it cheaper to get certain jobs done in this way rather than buy the expensive machinery required.

He glanced at the hedge, chatted about his schooldays sixty-odd years ago and how things had changed, and promised he'd send one of his men on Wednesday week; couldn't manage it earlier, not a machine available.

In the event, on the day appointed, we knew his promise was being kept long before the confirmation of our own eyes. The foundations of our little cottage shook, the surrounds trembled and groaned. My wife rushed out to find out what in the world was happening.

The tractor, almost the size of a tank, rumbled to a halt. I couldn't believe it. The driver apparently felt the same about the hedge or more precisely his only means of approach to it. Manoeuvring his chariot of war into position, he leaned out of the cab, smiled sickly, and mentioned he was afraid the lawn, such as it was, was going to get a little churned up.

Ah, the optimism of understatement!

Between a rose bush and the garden path he drove forward with sufficient care to restrict the number of craters bang in the middle of the green patch to no more

31

than four, and then launched his attack with the digger attachment.

The tractor driver was an artist, working the digger to within fractions of an inch to avoid bushes, flowers, the dovecot, a wall, the garden gate, everything in fact but the hedge itself as he removed the lot in less than ten minutes. Not only so, but still from his cab he tidied up the mess, dumping it out of sight, ready for burning. All that remained was to retire to the cottage for light refreshments.

He told us he left home every morning at first light, and never finished work until dark, often much later if the tractor's powerful headlights could pick out the job in hand.

Did he, we wondered, ever feel tempted to hire out his skills for more pay, building a motorway or something of the kind?

'I'm happy enough here,' he chirped, 'plenty of fresh air, nobody breathing down my neck, time to live,' he reached for a third cup of tea, 'what more could I want?'

'More money!' My wife was only half serious.

He roared with laughter, climbed into his cab, cheerfully added a few more craters as he backed to the dirt road, and was on his way to the next job – digging drains at a battery-hen farm, a place which we soon planned to visit for the nicest of reasons.

Meanwhile the conservationist in me couldn't help wondering . . .

'Isn't that an improvement!' My wife beamed at the empty space. 'All we need now is some fertilizer, give the soil a chance.' And for the next five minutes or so she enthused about transforming the area into a modest flower garden; to counter-balance, if nothing else, our preoccupation with vegetables and soft fruits.

Fertilizer!

Inevitably the law of association flashed my mind back to the conversation with the old shepherd – his reflections on the output of horses and donkeys. Furthermore, I recalled he'd mentioned a man not all that far from us whose passions in life – Shetland ponies – offered a growing mountain of proof of how much these tiny creatures ate, manure freely available to his neighbours for the asking.

'I wonder,' I said to my wife, 'what he does with his muck? The ponies'!' I sought to be explicit.

'I don't mind asking him,' she said. 'Nice man. I'm sure he won't mind sparing some for us.'

She picked up the phone, and Walter offered to drop off a tractor load at the garden gate. No trouble at all. As much as we wanted. For free, of course.

She thanked him for this avalanche of kindness, but thought a wheelbarrow full would be adequate. 'I'll get my husband to pop round,' I heard her say.

When I arrived Walter was standing with his father by the farmyard gate, the pair of them unmistakably country-men to their finger tips. Each possessed a face indicating either high blood pressure or – as in their case – weather-beaten rosiness.

'You've come for your wife's fertilizer!' Walter greeted me, his welcome reinforced by the older man's hand-shake. 'We heard you'd arrived,' he said, 'settling in all right?' Not waiting for an answer he pointed in the direction of a farm building. 'There it is,' he sounded encouraging, 'help yourself. Lovely stuff. Put hairs on your chest.'

My eyes followed his signal – and I gawped at a veritable Everest. 'How many ponies do you have?' I asked.

'Four at the moment,' he said.

My eyes again surveyed the steaming mass. 'Four!' I was astonished.

'The ponies didn't shit the lot.' Walter's blooming face remained serious. 'The bullocks help, and there's plenty of straw mixed with it. Beautiful for the garden, nothing better. Take as much as you want.'

I pushed the wheelbarrow to the foothills, adjusting my nostrils, wiped the rising ammonia from my eyes, and sank the fork deep. It was greeted by what sounded like bubbling or perhaps this was caused by my wellingtons slowly disappearing. Whatever the reason, the noise was like music, a hymn of thanksgiving for the wonders of farmyard manure.

Make no mistake, you can't buy this stuff at a gardening centre! By the time I reached home even the fork handle was beginning to grow. Mind you, the second load, despite Walter showing me what he called a short cut from his farmyard to our cottage, nearly killed me.

Next morning, struggling with a rigor-mortis back, I almost wished it had. And at the end of the day, the time of reputed harvest, I was compelled to recognize there's more to growing things than an abundance of quality fertilizer. Not that this could fairly be said of my wife's tomatoes. She was, I fear, eventually embarrassingly successful; embarrassing, that is, by comparison with my crop of walnut potatoes and stunted carrots.

Never mind, we were learning – and having lots of fun in the process. Mostly fun!

3

Doves, cats and the kiss of death

You might have gathered from the story of the bird in the chimney that we don't often have a fire in the lounge. There's no need. The Aga – apart from being superb for cooking – provides constant hot water which also heats the bathroom through a towel rail. In the lounge we have a paraffin heater; might sound primitive but in our experience it doesn't smell at all if the nozzle is kept clean and the wick trimmed. Into the bargain it's cheaper to run and adequate for the colder weather. Of course, we use the open fireplace on special occasions – anniversaries, birthdays, Christmas and the like, but even then the beloved Aga is indispensable.

Which, as night follows day, reminds me of the farm track outside our garden gate! With the occasional tractor passing our way it's peppered with holes, some of them small craters, deep enough to make walking an exercise in concentration, and also, more serious, an occasional hazard to wild life. We'll return to this in a moment.

Such holes outside the front door provide, no question, two distinct advantages, one practical, the other aesthetic. A quick downpour, and we have a series of bird baths, guaranteed entertainment for as long as we have time to watch. This morning, for instance, we were charmed by a blackbird launching itself, splashing with its wings, douching its soft feathers, drying itself with shakes and shimmies before gleefully starting the whole wild wallowing all over again.

The practical benefit? There's always somewhere to put

the ashes, no small undertaking with a heating system like ours. Indeed, without this steady supply of hole-filling material the bird baths would soon become small lakes, suggesting all manner of dire consequences.

Not long after we'd arrived, a five-year-old from the farmhouse rushed into our cottage to drag me fighting and struggling, never mind my favourite radio programme, to *see*. A bird apparently unable to fly, its wings bedraggled, hopping forlornly near a crater of water. Its repeated efforts to take off landed it once or twice in the water, adding to its helplessness and terror.

As we talked about what was best to do I was surprised – remembering my own reaction to the supposed death of the jackdaw in the lounge – at his mature attitude. There was no doubting his concern and compassion, but he knew and accepted that sometimes creatures suffered and died or had to be put down; accepted, in fact, that death, which inescapably he came across in field and hedgerow, was simply part of the cycle of life, neither surprising nor frightening.

But all this was before that never-to-be-forgotten weekend when we were left in charge of his and his younger sister's beloved cat, born a runt and kept alive against all the odds to become as much a part of the family as mum and dad!

Special for all the wrong reasons, this cat was a survivor, evidence that loving care is sometimes stronger than natural law. Despite excessive feeding, it was underweight, permanently stunted. Its eyes, one blue, the other brown – confirmation of pedigree breeding! – were almost constantly running, and, like its nose, in need of frequent bathing with warm water to remove the congealed mess. It was also a compulsive sneezer, spreading mucus on humans and furniture alike.

But its biggest handicap was mental. Here was a cat whose thought processes were decidedly slow; so slow as to be virtually non-existent. If it possessed a brain at all it was either damaged or addled at birth. Presumably it knew it was a cat, though every feline characteristic was conspicuous only by its absence, in total contrast to the other cat in the family, a marauding tom appropriately named Leo.

The latter's bluish-grey flowing coat made it appear even more enormous than its well-above-average proportions; from every standpoint a magnificent animal, and pompous with it, seemingly aware of the admiration, not to say fear, it evoked from all and sundry.

Leo never walked, always strutted like the uncrowned king he knew himself to be. I'd first met him in rather unfortunate circumstances! On leaving the city we'd been given a pair of doves by doubtless well-meaning friends, the idea being these reputed symbols of peace should constantly remind us of all the good wishes associated with our move to the country. It worked!

The doves survived their two-week habituation and cooed their pleasure at joining us in such a delightful setting.

In the fullness of time we watched nest building in the dovecot, the cock chasing the hen clearly with single-minded intent, and soon her near total disappearance to sit on the two eggs. As far as we could see she left them only once for daily feeding, and then for barely a couple of minutes.

The days slipped by, and we became caught up in the excitement of waiting for the emergence of the fledglings, our very own, guaranteed, we'd been told, to be a cock and hen.

Leo too was excited, for precisely the opposite reason.

Our thoughts were of life! Not that we overlooked the threat he represented. In the friendliest possible way we made it clear he should keep away from the vicinity of the dovecot; appealed to him, chased him, threw a ball at him (missed, of course), and stood guard against him at every waking moment.

All we achieved was to delay the dispatch of the first fledgling to emerge, for a whole twenty-four hours. We actually saw Leo take it, like a streak of lightning, and nip off with me in pursuit. In the light of what happened next I can't decide whether he was repentant or intimidated – a likely story! – or merely more interested in the hunting than the kill and its reward. For in response to my shouts he stopped running and meekly sat, fledgling in his mouth, apparently waiting for me to relieve him of his prey. It was still alive, but lasted no more than minutes, a sad end to all our waiting.

The problem was, we couldn't help but admire Leo. Or perhaps respect is the word. Certainly not love. Cats, I reckon, aren't lovable, being totally incapable of affection themselves. Their only interest in humans is to exploit them – take their devotion, their shelter, their food, without in any way, unlike a dog, offering loyalty and happy obedience in return.

Whoever saw a cat doing as it was told? Felines are a law unto themselves, purring their approval only at their own convenience. Yet I can't help, as I say, but admire cats like Leo, admire and respect them for their fierce independence and determination to be, notably in the country, not pets but cats. Beyond question there's something awe-inspiring about Leo on the prowl. At one time, still influenced by city sentimentality, I tried to protect his intended victims, shouting a warning, shooing him away, but not any more.

Leo's intended victims have their own intended victims; save the former and you condemn the latter. Nature's way is best – the survival of the fittest, separation of the quick from the dead.

Which inevitably, if rather circuitously, brings me back to the mentally-handicapped cat with running eyes and nose, and a built-in sneeze of enormous range. Luby, a name lovingly chosen for inscrutable reasons, was the exception to the rule in all manner of ways, not least in the universal love she commanded. I doubt whether there ever was a cat more unreservedly loved. And another exception – she herself appeared to have limitless capacity to love and show affection, frequently the way, I've noticed, with the mentally handicapped.

Much of her appeal was her sometimes uncatlike behaviour. For instance, I came across her shortly after spotting Leo stalking and killing a rabbit as big as himself, a rabbit, incidentally, which at least gave the impression of putting up a fight. Luby, also on the prowl, had firmly in her sights a butterfly!

What complicated the matter for the hunter was the hunted's predisposition not to stay still. The butterfly would land on the garden path, Luby would commence her stealthy approach, get within springing distance for the kill, and look startled as the butterfly flitted further up the path. Luby would try again. And again.

By now her face, like the futile waving of a paw at the once more airborne cabbage white, was a picture; a picture not merely of utter bewilderment but uninhibited joy. For even Luby appeared to be sharing the joke, the funny side of her ineptitude. And it *was* funny, without in any way making this lovable apology for a cat an object of ridicule. On the contrary, such incidents, and there were many, further endeared her to all and sundry, most of all the two children to whose family she belonged.

When holiday time arrived, despite all the excitement, they and their parents made no secret of their concern for Luby's welfare during their three-week absence. Leo was no problem. He was more than capable of looking after himself. Many a night after again satiating himself with the spoils of hunting he couldn't even be bothered to come home for breakfast, preferring to sleep off his blissful discomfort in a favoured secluded place – top of a garden shed reaching into a tree outside the kitchen door. Whatever happened, he, they knew, would be around at their return, possibly acknowledging it with suitable condescension as he received their plaudits at reunion.

Luby was something else. She definitely needed looking after – cherished, her nose wiped, her eyes washed; two meals daily, water always available, no milk.

Would we mind?

On the contrary, to have Luby around was, for reasons I've indicated, a pleasure; privilege. Even the doves didn't bat a feather. I swear they watched her hunting butterflies or daddy-long-legs, another of her favourites, with a wicked smile on their faces. Call it instinct or whatever, they ignored completely the threat she tried to exhibit, staying put at her approach, landing near her, presumably aware she was harmless, no more than a mouse in cat's clothing.

Luby's first few days with us were uneventful. True, the children's mother, separated from the family idol for as long as it takes to drive from our part of Kent to the Dover ferry, phoned to ask if the cat was surviving. Reassuringly, we could only admit she was. Just about.

During their absence we missed her once, only to find her after a frantic search curled up on a bale of hay in the ancient barn – still leaking a bit but as near draught proof

40

as makes no difference – probably exhausted after another sortie with a butterfly.

Fortunately, though we didn't have a cat, Hide 'n' Seek was fitted with a cat-flap, enabling Luby to come and go as she pleased. She seemed content, quick to jump on to any lap available, and exercise her bronchial purr at every opportunity. Endearing creature.

Saturday, the day *before* the quartet's return, dawned bright with promise. We fed the cats – Leo's helping totally ignored – and set about the inescapable chores of maintaining our Garden of Eden. Luby, we noticed, was stretched out in the garden, shaded from the already warm sun by a weeping willow planted since our arrival. Like her surroundings she looked peaceful.

We stopped for mid-morning coffee, heard a car approaching, and stepped out to welcome our visitors for the day. It was after the hugs and kisses, and exclamations of how lovely everywhere was looking, that my wife uttered a sort of stifled scream, nothing too alarming, just enough to suggest the end of the world.

We all followed her eyes. Luby was sprawled out, as far as I could see, still sun-bathing. In fact, one of our visitors, never having seen a cat so completely relaxed, facetiously suggested she looked out for the count. Everybody but my wife joined in the laughter. She ran across, her eyes full of anguish, and knelt by Luby.

What happened next is hard to capture in words. One of the visitors, a doting cat owner herself, started to massage Luby's heart. My wife picked up the phone and dialled the vet. He was out. His secretary advised we ascertain whether the cat was alive or dead.

Dead!

The phone conversation continued. Could we, my wife was frantic, bring the cat to the surgery? Just in case.

41

Perhaps it could be revived. The vet isn't here, his secretary repeated. But we must do something, my wife insisted. There's nothing we can do, the voice at the other end tried to calm the situation. You say the cat is dead. The vet can't bring it back to life. Even if he were here. And he isn't. No idea when he'll be back.

We must know what happened, my wife pleaded, *why* the cat has died. A post mortem? It won't help, the authoritative voice added to our consternation. In these circumstances, it went on, it's extremely difficult to discover the precise cause of death. Sounds like heart failure of some sort, but we really can't be sure. And whatever the reason, she brought the full weight of her matter-of-fact rationality to bear, it won't bring the cat back to life, will it?

There was, as they say, no answer to that!

My wife cradled the beloved cat entrusted to our care, cradled it with disbelief, still not convinced Luby was dead or rather struggling not to accept the undeniable. She stroked the still warm corpse, gently shook it, tried to breathe life into it, tenderly prised open its gungy eyes – all, of course, to no avail.

Our visitors rallied round uttering commiserations, helping us to decide what to do for the best, in view of the holiday-makers' return on the morrow. Even as we deliberated they were speeding from the South of France, doubtless keenly anticipating a joyous return and reunion.

Should we keep the cat for them to see? Or save them this trauma by burying Luby straightaway? Or approach another vet for a post mortem? Or seek a replacement in the twenty-four hours or so available to us? We were desperate. It wouldn't have been so bad, surely you understand, if the cat so much beloved had been our own. But our wretchedness was compounded by thoughts of our neighbours hurrying home. Then having to be told. The horror of that inescapable moment of truth followed us everywhere.

'Come on,' my still less than secure country realism tried to assert itself, 'let's see the thing in proportion. After all, it's only a cat! Imagine,' my voice trailed away, 'if it was one of the children . . .'

My wife's eyes withered me, silently shouted I didn't understand and was insensitive with it. What *about* the children, she murmured, will they think it's only a cat?

They know animals die, I sounded more confident than I felt. How many times have they seen dead hedgehogs and lambs and birds? Times without number, more in their short lives already than either of us put together. Undeterred I mentioned the bird with a broken wing the five-year-old had come across in the crater near our cottage, more dead than alive and doubtless grateful to be put out of its misery. Country children, I pontificated, are accustomed to such things. They understand. Alas, my words didn't silence the doubts nagging at the back of my mind as I contemplated the morrow.

Eventually, rightly or wrongly, we decided to bury Luby in a secret grave; secret, that was, unless those most directly concerned wished otherwise, our aim being simply to save them from further distress. A lovely spot was found under some trees, and we made preparations with the reverence of persons digging their own grave or planning their own funeral service.

We saw the car bouncing its way along the pitted farm track, and waited at the garden gate. Two excited children fell out, flung their arms round our necks, simultaneously asking about the cats, the departed by name. I tried to divert their attention by pumping them about their holiday, giving my wife the chance to break the news to their parents.

Leo sailed past in his majestic style, as indifferent to their return as their departure. The children attempted to express their delight, but managed only to chase him further beyond their grasp, leaving them free to concentrate on their reunion with Luby!

I glanced at the trio still at the car, and knew this was not going to be an easy day. The parents came inside, sipped coffee, pondering what to do for the best. Should they tell the children now or play for time, somehow preparing the way to lessen the blow? Their mother was more fearful of the older child's reaction, the five-year-old, my companion, as I've indicated, on many a brutal encounter with the laws of nature.

He was characteristically haring about the place, looking for Luby, almost falling into the pond, tripping over himself on the bricked garden path without a murmur, forgetting his grazed knee, and generally intimating that the holiday had done nothing to counter his whirlwind attitude to life.

His four-year-old sister, on the other hand, sat demurely on the settee, hugging her doll, her eyes darting between my wife and her mother, sensitive to the sombre atmosphere.

'Where's Luby?' she asked.

The parents and children disappeared into another room. We heard boyish sobs. Ten minutes later the four-year-old emerged fighting back her tears, emerged like a queen, marched across to my wife, climbed on to her lap, and brought the full weight of her childlike logic to bear.

'You!' she accused, 'killed Luby.'

My wife tried to explain. The little girl was adamant. 'You killed Luby!' she repeated, not nastily, rather with pity, sympathy. To her the case was clear cut. My wife had buried Luby, therefore my wife had killed her; buried, killed, what difference did it make! In the end it amounted to the same.

Securely settled on my wife's knee, this budding logician could not be persuaded otherwise. Meanwhile her brother was having his own battle trying to come to terms with the unacceptable. Forget the bird with the broken wing or the rabbit we'd found bloated with myxomatosis or another rabbit rotting in the middle of a field, a bullet through its head, or the dead shrews and pigeons and voles and field mice and doves. Forget the lot! All these he'd taken in his stride. The death of his own special pet belonged to another category altogether. He howled his protest at the harshness and futility of death.

His parents, not a little shattered themselves both with Luby's departure and the children's reaction to it, trying neither to under-estimate nor over-evaluate the significance of the calamity, encouraged the children to talk about it; and the four of them together decided that – all things considered – it wouldn't help in any way if they knew the whereabouts of the grave. Better for it to remain secret, not a constant reminder to reopen wounds each time they passed that way.

Such is the resilience of children, the wounds healed remarkably quickly without undermining in the least the mourners' devotion to the memory of the departed. As for the idea that my wife killed the cat, it appears to be the little girl's way of coping with the otherwise to her wholly inexplicable. Fortunately her reasoning also firmly keeps my wife as her 'best friend'.

A couple of weekends later we were confronted by another aspect of death the pair of us found even less acceptable than Luby's passing. We could look forward, a city friend assured us on the phone, to a different sort of meal, brought and prepared by her husband at Hide 'n' Seek. All *we* needed to do, she laughed at my mystification, was to sit back and eventually enjoy ourselves.

They arrived within the hour, he carrying a perk of his job – a massive crab and an even bigger lobster grabbed from the sea bottom as he ended his shift that afternoon as supervisor diver at a channel port. Couldn't be fresher, he brooked no argument, triumphantly displaying the animated victims.

Now we're rather partial to crab and lobster, but on this occasion an unexpected barrier suddenly stood between ourselves and this indulgence. To their credit our visitors broke the news with what I can only describe as stoical distaste – either we allowed them to cook the crab and lobster in the only way possible or denied both ourselves and them a meal to remember. There was, they continued to insist, simply nothing else for it.

I was appalled. My white-faced, disbelieving wife turned to her favourite cook book, consulted the index, and confidently started to read aloud:

'"A crab is usually sold ready cooked; in fact, many fishmongers will prepare and dress it as well. If it is bought alive, cook it as follows – wash it, place it in cold salted water, bringing slowly to boiling point, and boil fairly quickly for ten to twenty minutes."'

Her voice faltered. Not wasting a moment she reached for her tattered Mrs Beeton's, confident this dependable guide for long enough would bring not only enlightenment but vindication of her stand for humane cooking. Flipping the familiar pages, her eyes caught the top of the required column, and once more she defiantly began to read aloud:

'"Put the lobster into warm water, bring the water

gradually to the boil. This is believed by many to be a more humane method of killing, as the lobster is lulled to sleep and does not realize it is being killed."'

An alien thought crossed my mind. I wondered how Mrs Beeton were so sure, how she had gathered this inside knowledge of a lobster's feelings when being lulled to sleep in a pot of boiling water. My wife too appeared to share my doubt. Mrs Beeton's was, she said, perhaps a bit dated in some things. Better in this case to consult the very latest gourmet authorities, all of them surely paid-up members of the RSPCA.

She nipped along to the country cottage of a young city architect and his wife, happily in weekend residence, whose dinner parties reflect their library of international expertise and recipes. Cook them alive! The younger woman laughed at the very idea. Minutes later, her volumes sprawled over the kitchen table, she groaned her disbelief.

There was, the bemused supervisor diver tried to sound encouraging, one other way some people think less gruesome, even benevolent. He searched for words. You . . . you sort of, he laughed nervously, never more serious, you sort of pierce an eye with a screwdriver, and scramble the brain. Instantaneous death, he promised.

The trouble was, he felt the need to be honest, it's a bit dicey if you pierce at the wrong angle and miss the brain completely.

In a flash, being a sensitive type himself, wide open to the finer susceptibilities of man and beast, he saw his proposed option was less than universally acceptable, and helpfully diverted our attention by returning us to the impeccable Mrs Beeton's altogether more humane method of lulling the lobster to sleep by only gently boiling the water.

With this new insight into why natives with finer feelings always cooked their missionaries slowly, we eventually settled for barbecued chicken, still wondering what in the world to do with the crab and lobster. Needless to say, they remained as lively as proverbial crickets, rock safe behind the barrier of our hitherto unrealized objection to their being lulled to sleep.

Who was it said that civilization can be judged not by its works of art but how it treats its animals? I've no idea; but in any case, confronted by the need to cook crab and lobster rather than prise their succulence from a tin, I for one abruptly discovered I was allergic to both.

There is, however, one reputed concession to their finer feelings. True, it doesn't do much for their flavour, guaranteed by slower boiling, and the colouring suffers too, just a little, but who cares if the crab's or lobster's call to higher service on our behalf is made that much easier!

Bring the water to the boil, piping hot, and then, not a moment before, plunge the victim in head first. Our deep-sea diver friend and his wife assure us it cooks the brains in a trice, almost before the crab or lobster knows what's happening.

Perfectly humane, they insist.

4

The grave digger's (and Nature's) reverence for life

I had heard of a village nine or ten miles away which has the reputation for being one of the most picturesque in Kent, so – already addicted to long tramps on my own, the only way, I've discovered, to see wildlife and paradoxically to get to know countrymen – I set out to see for myself.

Long before I arrived, approaching from a meandering lane that seemed to go on forever, I could spot the church steeple, centre of the village. Adjacent was the churchyard, heavily sprinkled with ancient tombstones, and it was as I wandered among these examining the epitaphs that spadefuls of flying earth drew my attention to the as yet invisible worker.

He peered over the rim of the grave as I approached, decided it was time for a mid-morning break, and clambered out, seemingly anxious to pass the time of day.

'Yes, this job gets a bit lonely,' he agreed, rubbing his hands on his trousers and reaching for his knapsack to pour steaming tea from a flask. 'Sorry I can't offer you a cup,' he smiled; 'only enough for this and my dinner break.'

Having sipped a little, he unwrapped a sandwich of doorstep proportions, appeared to adjust his teeth, and sank them into oozing lemon curd. It looked as appetizing as his relish sounded.

We sat in silence, he eating and sipping, I taking in the scene of this ancient burial place, and also admiring, if that's the word, the skill of his work. Until now I'd imagined a grave digger simply dug a hole; an unhurried look indicated otherwise.

He told me he'd been digging graves most of his working life, and enjoyed the work. Enjoyed? Well, it was healthy, he explained, and important, he emphasized, a job calling for graft and respect.

'I remember,' he laughed, 'someone will dig my grave one day. You never know when your time's up.'

I could only agree; and wondered whether or how often the graves he prepared were for individuals he knew personally.

'More often than not,' he said; 'makes my job personal, if you see what I mean,' he murmured, subdued.

His attitude surprised me. I'd spoken to a grave digger, two or three, in fact, admittedly some years ago in the city, and couldn't fail to notice their down-to-earth approach, the refusal to get emotionally involved, somewhat akin to the professionalism required of doctor and nurse caring for the terminally sick. All very understandable.

This grave digger, still joyfully battling with his lemon curd sandwich and sipping his tea, suggested otherwise. He pointed out various graves of people he'd known, some of them his friends. He indicated an old beech tree overlooking a stone wall to rolling farm land.

'Over there,' he said, 'we laid Tom Whetstone to rest; full of years, ninety-one, as nice a man as you'd wish to meet. Worked on a farm all his life, till his retirement ten years back; that's right,' he felt the need to confirm, 'eighty-one when he finally moved to this village to live with his married daughter after she lost her husband. Tragic that was, too,' his eyes moved to another grave, 'killed by a tractor rolling on top of him.'

'Over there,' he pointed to the far corner, a magnificent

yew tree for sentinel, 'you'll find the old blacksmith's grave. Lived here all his life, born, bred, married and died in the same cottage. See what's on the stone,' he returned his flask to the knapsack, dropped into the nearly finished hole he was digging, and wished me good morning, my dismissal as courteous as it was absolute.

I approached the blacksmith's grave indirectly, taking in the last resting place of an extended family going back for generations, an imposing vault, parts of it struggling to stay visible under a jungle of briars, and a lonely cross carrying the name of a seven-year-old girl.

The blacksmith's epitaph was four words:

Gone With The Wind

Puzzled, not sure whether this was a medical diagnosis, theological statement or spiritual aspiration, I noticed the date – 1876. Then how come the grave digger had spoken as though he'd known the blacksmith personally? Perhaps he'd meant the blacksmith's father? Or brother? Or could it be I'd got the wrong grave?

I shall never know, for when I returned to ask I found only the grave digger's coat. After ten minutes or so of waiting I turned homeward, hopeful of still being in time for a ploughman's lunch at a pub on the boundary of the village. A taste for alcohol has always eluded me, but pub food is more to my liking than the poshest restaurant.

Strangely enough, as I discovered shortly after placing my order for home-made bread and goat's cheese, I wasn't done yet with what I was finding to be less than a morbid preoccupation with man's Last Enemy. A thud on the window behind me compelled attention, and there was a chaffinch out for the count.

Confidently, shadow of our chimney bird dancing in my mind, I waited for it to come round, shake itself, and fly away. Instead, while the casualty continued to show no sign of life, another chaffinch presumably its mate, swooped down, cocked its head to get a better view, seemed bewildered, and took off to a nearby tree from where it continued to stare. Within ten seconds it was back, chirping loudly, apparently trying to communicate with the ko-ed bird.

These flurries continued for perhaps ten minutes, the inspecting bird hopping round with growing agitation, flying away, coming back, chirping spasmodically, gazing intently upon its still inert partner, and finally taking off not to return, convinced the situation was hopeless.

I strolled outside and picked up the corpse, its body warm, its head flopping on a broken neck, indicating instantaneous death on impact. Otherwise it was unmarked, a riot of colours, each one complementing the others, the whole indescribably beautiful.

Yet in this case also pathetic, a further nudge to my already outraged feelings. Totally irrational. It wasn't the manner of the bird's death – after all, 'nature, red in tooth and claw', I'd seen far worse – but the stark incongruity of this incredible loveliness and death itself struck me as an affront, almost obscene. (Many months of further country wear and tear were to pass before I could accept such accidents with anything like the equanimity of a true countryman. In truth, I sometimes wonder whether I shall ever wholly manage it.)

On this occasion I lingered in the pub garden, feeling the structure of the wings, stretching the feathers to their full span, looking again at the colours, fingering the soft breast, the feet, the beak, the head.

Hearing my name called to collect the bread and cheese, I slipped the bird into my pocket, not sure at the time why, perhaps wanting – shades of the city – to ensure a decent burial.

But walking home I knew what to do, knew as sure as now I'm recalling that precise moment of realization. This bird must *not* be buried. Nature herself was too wise for such expressions of respect. The corpse must simply be returned to the on-going cycle of life – feathers to build nests and provide comfort, flesh to feed hungry mouths, bones eventually to enrich the soil, all to be used, never to die.

Perhaps you smile! Why the fuss about something so elementary and self-evident? All I can answer is that to me at the time it didn't seem either elementary or self-evident at all. Rather a revelation or a sort of mystical experience, if this doesn't sound too pompous.

No matter, as with reverence I laid the tiny corpse deep in the woods and took my leave, I felt part of the great re-cycling process, and this thought buoyed me along as the colours of the dead chaffinch continued to enliven my imagination.

The rest of the walk home was something of a pilgrimage, I don't know how else to put it. Not for a moment do I wish to suggest I understood, understand or subsequently found it easier always to accept the ways of nature, but I did and do feel part of the great scheme of things whose fundamental aim is life, an aim not contradicted but served even by the premature death of a chaffinch.

Such thoughts occupied me as I approached the circumference of the woods within sight of Hide 'n' Seek. Could I hear voices, angry and threatening, shattering the peace of all this loveliness? I quickened my step, no longer in doubt. And what I found added another dimension to my less-than-starry-eyed understanding of country life. And people.

We had new neighbours, arrivals of no more than a month back. Neighbours? Well, only a few fields separated us, and already we were on more than nodding acquaintance. They were life-long country folk transferring from one part of the Garden of England to another, transferring reluctantly but needing space to expand, and hoping to enjoy the greater isolation. With them, among much else for mention at the appropriate time, they brought some exceedingly rare breeds of bantams, adored birds, little less than worshipped. To overhear these exotic creatures being discussed was to recognize that here was an affair not of the pocket only (they were very pricey) but the heart.

The bantams themselves strutted, never merely walked, obviously aware of their rarity and consequent value. They lived like royalty, displayed themselves accordingly at shows and exhibitions, and brought forth of their own kind with sufficient sparsity to guarantee inflated prices for each and every chick. To say their owners doted upon them is a cruel understatement.

I must say, they looked magnificent, justifiably a source of pride and pleasure; tiny birds with giant aspirations, peacocks of the farmyard, this particular farmyard. The first time I was allowed to gaze upon them I wasn't sure whether inwardly to cross myself or merely bend the knee. They were, believe me, that impressive. And their impact on first-time viewers was heavily reinforced by our neighbours' deference in their company.

Not too far away, other neighbours, no less charming and helpful, kept – until a fox discovered their address – not bantams, but an equally rare breed of chickens (Plymouth Rock, I believe, or something similarly obscure). More permanent members of their family were

54

two cockers, thoroughbreds, of course, as splendid in their way as the bantams in theirs.

Now we are, as you have surely realized pages back, a happy little community, mutually helpful and tolerant, sufficiently distant geographically from each other to make every contact pleasurable. So when the bantams moved in, the owners of the cockers, characteristically wanting to be helpful, and knowing the built-in proclivities of their dogs through long breeding, set about reinforcing the fences between themselves and the miniature peacocks.

The dogs were to keep to their patch, the bantams to theirs, a perfectly straightforward arrangement seeing that the owners of the dogs admired the bantams, and the owners of the bantams the dogs. Harmony was the order of the day. Every day. Until the cataclysm that occurred as I returned to Hide 'n' Seek, lost in thought about the chaffinch.

I started to run. Surely my ears were deceiving me? The voices sounded so heated and harsh. Was that a scream? A howl? A groan? Then I saw. Oh, my god!

I ran faster, gasping for breath. Hoping my eyes, like my ears, were deceiving me. But the growing evidence could not be denied.

Five dead bantams, one still in the mouth of the younger cocker, surrounded by neighbours clearly finding if difficult to maintain the customary bonhomie of our secluded community.

The dog dropped the bird, and wisely did a bunk. The wife of the bantams' owner picked up the corpse, then another, and a third, held up the bloody trio for all to see, and sloshed them in the direction of the face of the wife of the cocker's master.

Feathers began to fly. Threats ripped the air. Profuse

apologies were met with disbelief; disbelief, I imagine, not about the sincerity of the apologizer, but the devastation wrought in the twinkling of an eye by one normally playful dog.

Needless to say, the fence keeping the birds in or the dogs out was heavily reinforced; and harmony, if not entirely restored, was at least judiciously simulated.

5

The man with frozen carrots for fingers

A few days after the cocker and bantams outrage, I was walking to the village and noticed a cottage tucked away almost out of sight. It wasn't, however, the cottage that first caught my eye, but the front garden early ablaze with primulas and daffodils plus what looked to me like cultivated bluebells.

I stopped to feast my eyes, a new experience for me as far as flowers were concerned. Naturally I'd admired them often before in the city, frequently taking a bunch home from railway station or pavement florist, but this was altogether different, not unrelated to the astonishment rarely far away since our move.

Out of the cottage stepped a man who was – though little did I realize it at the time – soon to contribute considerably to my initiation into the more subtle wiles and wisdom of country living. This first time I saw him he was – like the vast majority of country people in my experience – slow in everything but the uptake.

Believe me, the days of the bumpkin, the simpleton who works on the land, have gone forever, always supposing they ever existed. If it suits the countrymen's purpose for outsiders from town and city to think them stupid, they're happy for the misinformation to linger; might deliberately add to the impression for their own amusement.

But they're slow only in the sense of being unhurried, reflecting their harmony with the rhythms of nature. Whatever the provocation to the contrary they take their time, confident they'll get there all the quicker by plodding not sprinting.

The cottager in his garden was a perfect illustration. Having nodded his agreement the flowers looked somewhat special, he took a tin from his trousers, leisurely rolled himself a cigarette, all the time, I was aware, sizing me up, not yet sure my interest wasn't threatening. Barely said a word.

He lit the malformed fag, spat out a stray piece of tobacco, demonstrated his rasping bronchial cough, muttered he shouldn't smoke really but didn't intend to give it up, and eventually, presumably convinced I wasn't out to do him down, invited me round the back to inspect his vegetable garden.

What really broke the ice between us – almost! – was the appearance of his grandson, clearly the apple of his eye, whose emergence from the cottage was heralded by a couple of Jack Russells yapping their delight.

The lad told them to be quiet, they instantly obeyed, and he disappeared to the garden shed. Meanwhile his grandad's gentle eyes of steel continued to scrutinize my very soul; not unfriendly, you understand, just the caution of a fundamentally kindly countryman not quite convinced I could be trusted.

His grandson returned and, perfectly at ease, precociously became part of our hitherto largely silent conversation. The difference was, the boy wanted to talk, and proved remarkably articulate, notably about space travel, clearly his obsession. He listed the names not only of both American and Russian astronauts but their back-up teams, rattled them off as I at his age talked about star footballers. The old man glowed with pride.

The two of us alone again, he mentioned how his grandson's bedroom – he lived with his grandparents –

was plastered with pictures and diagrams of space travel; and then he told me about a letter he'd recently received from the village school asking him to get in touch with the headmaster.

Not a little put out by such an official communication, confident, whatever the trouble, his grandson was innocent, he wasted no time in presenting himself.

To his consternation he was received like royalty!

Did he realize, the headmaster wanted to know, that this grandson of his was outstanding, head and shoulders above the other pupils, one of the most capable youngsters he had ever been privileged to teach?

The cottager's face as he told me was a study. His eyes twinkled, his smile grew; even the extending dew-drop on the end of his nose, finally resting on the drooping fag, added to the pleasure of his recital.

Would he, the headmaster wanted to know, allow his grandson to be nominated for a scholarship at a famous public school, all expenses paid including ample pocket money for a boy in such circumstances? All that was required was the family's agreement for the application to go ahead.

The proud countryman went back to his humble cottage where long into the night the matter was discussed, not, he said, without constant reminders the whole idea wasn't a dream, a fantasy. *His* grandson go to the most famous public school in the land! But that's what the headmaster had seriously proposed, and he'd asked for an answer as quickly as possible.

Yes, but would the lad be happy? Wouldn't he feel a misfit, almost a freak in such a setting? And what happened when his posh education came to an end? The old man and his wife didn't know, only feared the lad might

59

be confused about where he belonged, cut off from his roots, neither one thing nor another.

On the other hand, what a chance . . .

To make a decision wasn't easy, but, eventually the cottager returned to the village school. Thank you very much, he told the headmaster, but we think he'll be better off staying here with us. If he's as bright as you say he'll do well at the comprehensive, and can work it out for himself from there. Rest assured we'll give him all the support he needs. The kindly headmaster didn't try to hide his disappointment. And as the old countryman made his way home he simply hoped the right decision had been made. As for the boy himself, as I now have every reason to know, he continues to be one of the most happy and carefree youngsters anyone could wish to meet.

No doubt at all, such a loving home in a village like ours is bound to teach an inquisitive child lots of desirable things not on the curriculum of a public school, no matter how famous. Even so, I could see the old countryman wasn't without his regrets; confident he'd made the right decision in the boy's best interests, sad at the same time it couldn't be otherwise.

'If he's as clever as they say he is,' he concluded, 'who knows where he might finish up? It's up to him.'

We resumed talking about the garden, back and front. Talking? His every reluctant word belied our easy exchanges of the previous five minutes, returning us to mutual awkwardness. I moved towards the gate, cast a final appreciative glance at the flowers, and thanked him for the chat.

'You don't, by any chance, want to buy a cow? Beautiful milker, a Jersey, reared it myself, lovely temperament.'

We both laughed, he doubtless at my astonished reaction, I at the ludicrous idea. Me – buy a cow, beautiful milker or not! I was still laughing when I told my wife. 'What would we do with a cow?' I said, confident of immediate agreement.

'Might be fun!' she said.

And, love help us, the woman was serious, brushing aside my exclamations.

'You,' she reminded me, 'were sold on the idea of a couple of goats. What's the difference?'

My mouth fell open in punctured protest.

'At least it's worth thinking about.' Her reasonableness was infuriating.

'A housecow!' I declared, imagining the emphasis itself would illustrate the lunacy.

'If *I*,' she smiled, 'am prepared to milk two goats, one housecow should be a walkover. Shouldn't it?' Her voice turned the question into a reprimand.

I couldn't believe it! This city girl to her finger tips who still occasionally talked nostalgically of pavements and street lights and a lavatory connected to the mains and – most ominous of all – the stimulating hurly-burly of London, seriously telling me she was prepared to milk a housecow. Did the woman realize the implications? Twice a day, seven days a week, fifty-two weeks a year – gallons and gallons of milk, running out of our ears.

'A housecow would be nice.' She had a faraway look in her eyes.

The following weekend I retraced my steps to the old countryman's cottage. He wasn't in, but his wife, villager like her husband from birth, directed me to a small-holding half-a-mile or so from their cottage.

My approach was heralded long before my arrival by a growling, snarling, unnerving-looking beast. True, the creature was on a lead, but its ambition was clearly the removal of at least one of my legs, and it was struggling to get nearer.

Now what was it the cottager had already imparted at our first meeting, wisdom prompted by his yapping Jack Russells? Never let a dog smell your fear. Let it know who's boss. Otherwise it will seek to oust you as pack leader.

Fair enough! Boldly, I climbed the gate, circumspectly beyond the defender's length of lead. The dog went mad. With equal boldness I was just about to nip back over the gate, when a stentorian command told 'the silly bugger' to be quiet. Instant peace.

I glanced over my shoulder and saw a tail between two legs disappearing into a half-beer-barrel kennel. The cottager strolled across, gave the dog a session of ear kneading, let it off the lead, and the three of us, the dog crazy with delight, made our way to a building of indescribable character, seemingly defying nothing more than the law of gravity.

Surprisingly the inside was solid and snug, and no less sweet smelling for the presence of half-a-dozen pigs or rather piglets almost ready, I gathered, for village deep freezers. As the old countryman climbed into the pen, the porkers advanced towards him, frantic to give him a welcome, or so it seemed, wrestling among themselves for the privilege of having their backs scratched, piggy ecstasy.

He told me he obtained them from a neighbouring pig farm between four and six weeks, if possible from the same sow which produced three litters a year. He took the little 'uns from among the thirty to forty she produced annually, confident they would quickly come on with the ample rations of milk he was able to make available.

Sows come into season within days of farrowing, requiring the immediate availability of boar or AI (artificial insemination). Only people, he chuckled, are capable of sex all the year round. With stock, he affectionately patted one of the pigs on the backside, you've got to catch 'em in season; no use otherwise, they won't want to know.

We walked across to his ferrets and hens and assortment of pigeons and doves. His two cows, mother and daughter, the former a family pet for years, were grazing, reminding me of the main reason for my visit. You're too late, he responded, I've found a buyer, a family new to the district wanting a housecow. I felt more reprieved than relieved.

Suddenly the sun came out, lifting my spirits, making me freshly aware of all the loveliness as far as my eyes could see.

By now we'd reached the gate for me to take my leave. I assured him he was always welcome to pay us a visit at Hide 'n' Seek, and responding to his evident interest in the idea tried to explain how to find us. If you're walking, I concluded, you can take a short cut through the woods.

'You mean by Hermit's Place?' he queried.

My face must have registered both surprise and interest, for he immediately took up the story where the woodman had left off.

At the turn of the century, when everybody who lived in the village also worked in or near it, a widow and her son occupied a cottage on the heath. The son, only twelve when his father died ten years before, was, and had always been, a loner, the odd one out.

He hated school, left before his time, and eventually became a gamekeeper, feared by every poacher in the neighbourhood. He hated them all at least as much as they detested him, and, being good at his job, was often responsible for their appearance before the magistrates. Needless to say, he was just about the most unpopular person for miles around, which probably explains why he never married, content to live with his mother.

She was by all accounts a proud little body, asking for and expecting nothing from anyone, maintaining her independence largely by taking in washing from the big houses, and keeping some of them as spotless as her little cottage.

One night – summer, it was, very hot, dry – he untypically called in at the pub on his way from the woods, and coming out met a man going in he hadn't seen since they were kids at school, a soldier home on leave. They talked about old times, shared a few rounds, and left the pub together.

Next morning, nursing a hangover, the gamekeeper was late for work, frantic he might be found out. He heard a movement in the woods, followed his ears, and braced himself, fully expecting to be confronted by the boss.

The cottager paused, smiled, waiting for effect, his timing doubtless perfected by much telling of this bit of local folklore. His face creased with the merry roguishness of a cat playing with a mouse.

Through the trees, he brought himself to continue, the gamekeeper saw what caused his heart to beat faster. Two policemen, one the village copper and friend of nearly all, stealthily approaching like poachers themselves. And they'd found their prey – the gamekeeper. Come with us, they said.

I was captivated, hook, line and sinker; the old countryman knew it, and continued his silent teasing. At last he released two words with the reluctance of a monk vowed to silence.

Circumstantial evidence!

Yes, but about what?

The crime, he sucked each word like a piece of chocolate, was MURDER.

The post-mistress, Maud, spinster of this parish, had been found with her head battered in. The gamekeeper and his soldier pal, reputedly the worse for drink, had been seen near the scene of the crime, the village post office, not far from the pub. The police wanted, as they say, to eliminate them from their enquiries.

By all accounts they had one hell of a job proving they hadn't done it. Suspicion centred on 'em for ages, in fact, never did go away, probably 'cause they never did find the murderer. Rum old business, don't you think!

In the end, the gamekeeper couldn't stand the stares and whispers in the village; so when his mother died shortly afterwards, killed by the worry, I shouldn't wonder, he took himself off to live in a shack deep in the wood. Rarely showed his face again, as though he didn't exist. A proper hermit.

Hence Hermit's Place, I brought my city logic to bear.

No, no, the countryman celebrated my wrong conclusion.

As before he was in total command of his timing, whimsically dangling me on a piece of string, his eyes almost laughing themselves out of their sockets.

They found him dead, stiff as a beanpole. Natural causes, they said. Natural causes, my arse! he commented. Big fella like that, strong as a bull like gamekeepers had to be in them days. He didn't die of no natural causes!

He started to laugh; well, smile, his face contradicting his sombre words. Hermit's Place, he said, is where they found the body. If you're going home that way you'd better watch out. They do say it's haunted. Mark you, he sounded apologetic, I've seen nothing myself; but that's as likely 'cause I ain't been that way for years. To tell you the truth, it used to give me the creeps.

Amused at such superstitious nonsense, I took my leave determined to go that way round, wondering exactly where the body was found, puzzled no one else had mentioned the shack, never mind the corpse. Deeper in the woods, nearing the imagined spot, I felt the need inexplicably to keep glancing over my shoulder, startled by familiar noises now sounding sinister.

Ghost stories leave me cold. This one was warming me up – irrationally, unforgivably – not least because I found my step increasing. Nothing excessive, just the leisurely charge of a body drenched with adrenalin.

Once out of the woods, my customary scepticism about such matters returned me to sanity, and I completed my walk fuming against the idiocy of tales of the supernatural. The only reason I haven't been back to that part of the woods since is my preference for the scenery the longer way round.

Over the next few weeks I often watched the old country-man, seated on a three-legged stool, his head pushed against the haunches of his beloved remaining Jersey, working his fingers to transfer her gallons to his bucket, no trouble at all. Yet when I tried, the squirt became a trickle, and in no time my hands ached.

'You get used to it,' the old countryman laughed, holding up his fingers to demonstrate their strong supple-ness, remarkable for a man of his years.

His daily routine never varied. Early morning and late afternoon he greeted his Jersey cow as though she were a returning prodigal, and muttered endearments as her bulging udder was unburdened. Surplus milk he fed to the pigs. Much of the rest his wife turned into butter which, I can testify, was delicious, as much as the pints of cream I sometimes took home.

You couldn't wish to meet a happier or more contented couple, I can tell you; hard working, proudly independent, generous, unfailingly ready to lend a hand, no fuss. He spent much of his time at their small-holding and if he wasn't tending the animals he was engaged in a bit of country wheeling and dealing, as much for his personal interest as any profit. She baked bread, churned butter, pottered in the garden, and – as she was fond of saying – counted her blessings.

When his arms, then hands and fingers, began to ache and tingle, just a little, nothing, he said, hardly worth a mention, he poked fun at himself for getting old before his time, and confidently expected to throw *it* off (whatever *it* was) by yesterday!

Knowing him better than the back of her hand, his wife casually dropped the hint it might be a good idea for him to pop into the doctor's, when he happened to be passing, no need to worry or fret. He agreed. But never seemed to pass that way.

Milking by now was little short of masochism.

It would be wrong to give the impression this wise old man was either obstinate or stupid. Like the rest of us he didn't take kindly to pain; but he can't abide doctors or more correctly going to the doctor's, firmly convinced that to do so is half-way to persuading yourself you're ill. This philosophy might explain why he claims never to have had a day's illness in his life!

Alas, the pain in his fingers persisted, turning them into frozen carrots, finally compelling him to visit the village surgery.

The diagnosis? Arthritis, in this case part of the ageing process, decidedly incompatible with milking twice daily.

Already the beloved Jersey has gone to what her former owner calls 'a good home' by which he simply means she will definitely not go to slaughter but continue to be treated as a member of a family.

Even so, the parting has rocked this old countryman's world; not the going of the cow herself, for, to one inured to such sentimentality, she was replaceable, but the very foundations of his whole life-style – routine of morning and afternoon milking, nurturing his pigs, meeting his stock's essential needs; the sense of having work that must be done, of being his own man.

Piece by piece the result of years of hard toil is silently collapsing round his ears, barely noticed by most of the village. A death without a corpse? Not that he, any more than his wife, will give up easily, but both are agreed that arthritic fingers don't help!

Knowing them as I do, I imagine and hope that this imperceptible tragedy will prove nothing more than a turn in the road leading to new interests and achievements. We shall see.

6

Village nobs and commoners

More certain was a discovery my wife made about herself shortly after arriving here and progressively as the months slipped by. To what extent this was initiated by endless rain for days, turning the countryside not flooded into a mud bath I can't say. All I know for sure is that after the car was stuck in this quagmire and returned to the farm track only following much digging, heaving, cursing and other things not guaranteed to cement a happy marriage, she discovered she possessed legs, a complete pair, two in fact.

The revelation was little short of cataclysmic. For starters she decided to walk to her new job in the village, a mere two-and-a-half miles, almost unbelievable for someone never previously tempted to walk beyond the nearest bus stop, underground station or taxi. The route, need I remind you, was little short of battle training.

Shortly after first light she moved along the path to our gate, crossed a field, through the farmyard, across another field, over the first cattle grid, across another field, over the second cattle grid, across two more fields, over the third cattle grid, before the final three hundred strides to the tarmac road.

All that now remained between her and her destination was a half mile to the village pub, or one of them, a further mile right through the village, and some two hundred more strides from the village green to the office.

She loved it. Never felt so fit for years, if ever. Agreed – as she was the first to admit – this wasn't saying much, but the claim lacked nothing in the telling. The weather

69

didn't seem to matter. Rain, wind or storm, she set out with relish, and insisted never to have been either disappointed or inconvenienced, never mind the occasional soaking. There was so much new to see. In other words she was introduced to things unavoidably hidden to car travellers, a different perspective altogether, as I too was increasingly learning.

Often we walked through the village together, an education in itself, sometimes for unexpected reasons. It didn't take us long to realize that – without drawing too precise a line – our little community consisted of two social groups – the commoners and the nobs. The latter tended to favour one end of the village, clustered together like bees round hives of inflated price, the top end, the old village, more grand, impressive, and prosperous in ways self-evident in the country. The gardens were bigger or at least much neater, with more flowers than vegetables. The lawns were greener, often manicured to perfection.

Commoners lived at the bottom end, incorporating a rambling housing estate and also a charming assortment of tiny cottages once inhabited by farm labourers and the like.

Cars owned by the nobs occupied garages; at the bottom end they were parked on the road. Paint work and general appearance at the top end were immaculate; at the bottom sometimes less so.

This fixed social divide, no more acknowledged than ignored, was reflected in the village's dogs. The nobs tended to go in for extremities, Mastiffs and/or Pekineses, the rarer or more exotic the breed the better. Commoners, on the other hand, though partial to the occasional Alsatian, consorted with sheepdogs, whippets, Jack Russells or, most common of all, unfortunate mating consequences.

In the city I was hardly aware of dogs. I saw some, of course, usually nosing garbage bins for survival, but beloved city dogs functioned behind closed doors or in providing daily exercise for their owners.

In the country, things were somewhat different. Dogs were more common than cars. A few worked for their living. Some were kept for hunting not foxes but rabbits and rats. More, if not most, were guard dogs, though no one could imagine that our neck of the woods was a hotbed of criminal activity.

All dogs were accepted, even by non-dog owners, as part of the scene. The problem was, some of we newcomers with urban backgrounds were still in the process of transmogrification! It was too tempting for us to think of dogs as status symbols, a means of registering our place in the social pecking order. And there are occasions when a city upbringing is not the best preparation for the care of the most devoted canine addition to the family. This was brought home to me by a villager with roots deep in the soil who swore the story was true, an eye-witness account.

He was strolling across the village green, minding his own business, set on making a simple purchase at the village shop. Along came a lady dripping with affluence, at her feet a Pekinese, the pair of them eyes only for each other. The dog cocked its legs once or twice, and then obliged by getting down to solid excretions, clearly the main purpose of the outing.

Its ecstatic owner cooed her congratulations and pulled from her handbag – it's God's truth, my informant at this point felt it necessary to interject – what at first looked like a paper handkerchief. Tenderly she bent down to the dog and wiped its backside, finally dropping the piece of toilet paper into a carrier bag carrying the name of a famous supermarket, and marching off triumphantly, the shit on the village green a monument to her concern for her pet's cleanliness.

'Bloody visitors,' he concluded.

His concern about 'visitors' was centred upon one or two new settlers among the nobs who apparently found it difficult to refer to the commoners by other than their surnames. Yet they, I was growingly informed, not only expect but take as their God-given right a deferential manner of address. Who the bloody hell do they think they are!

With my egalitarianism imbibed from the city, I suggested the answer was obvious, answer like with like, but this was, I now better appreciate, totally to under-estimate the countryman's natural courtesy. My informant, member of the parish council, champion upholder of the rights of every villager, nobs and commoners alike, beloved father and grandfather and community godfather, was no more capable of referring to his fellow councillors by their surnames than complaining to their faces when the nobs among them showed less than this politeness to him.

Not that anybody can say we're not an all-pull-together village, despite any social or political divide. At election times, for instance, most of us paint our homes blue, one way or another; a few of us display our SDP posters; a handful of us run the gauntlet and support the Labour Party. Yet when for the umpteenth time inevitably the Tory candidate is returned with a thumping majority nobody bats an eyelid or shows the slightest bad grace.

Every year a Labour Party activist organizes a public strawberry and cream tea for party funds, and you should see the members or supporters of all the parties tucking in, indifferent that their money is swelling the coffers of the dreaded enemy. Village democracy at its best.

Naturally, come the morning after, we all happily revert to our respective political dug-outs. As one villager was overheard to say: 'How do we get these buggers out?' But even if he were serious, he was speaking only for himself. The rest of us are ardently committed to the politics of our gardening society – put more into the soil (and the bank) than you take out.

Working the soil, indeed, work of any kind, reminds me that increasingly these days it's an over-simplification to differentiate between villagers born and bred here and the increasing number of newcomer commuters. More and more locals too are commuting; either this or moving into an urban area, driven there looking for work, hating the necessity but reconciled to it long before they leave school.

Not so long ago, agriculture and horticulture found openings for any youngster wanting to work on the land. These days, what with mechanization and intensive farming, such opportunities are drastically reduced. And even some of those who do manage to get a foot in this rapidly closing door often soon become disenchanted, reluctantly uprooting themselves from the village for richer pickings elsewhere or – much more frequent – simply to find somewhere to live when they want to get married.

We saw this latter necessity in the process of working itself out shortly after starting our Saturday afternoon explorations of the neighbourhood. Stumbling across cricket on the village green, a game of what proved to be friendly belligerence between our village and another with the contradictory name of Great Sapling, my wife and I settled to watch. Charmed.

Suddenly the church bells began to go crazy. And soon we saw a horse-drawn carriage driven by a flowing beard in Victorian coachman's uniform, conveying a radiant bride and presumably her father to her wedding. Shyly she spared a royal wave to the knots of villagers standing along the way.

She was, we subsequently learned, a third generation villager, member of the squash club, basket ball team and drama group, main elements within her hectic social life all centred on the village hall or green, wanting like her bridegroom from the next village to continue to commute to work in the nearest town.

Yet their wedding day marked their departure from the area; first-time buyers stand little chance in this setting these days. The only way they could find a reasonably priced home was to uproot themselves; another nail, as an old villager expressed it to us, in the coffin of our village's chances of survival.

Of course, the village will survive all right, no question. The list of potential buyers waiting to snap up property in the area grows apace. But the old villager's concern was the changing nature of the village, the way people like us, transfers or escapees from the concrete jungle, inadvertently sometimes drive away individuals born here and wanting to stay.

No wonder some of the older villagers, clinging to each other for the security of their common roots, guardians of a way of life they believe in danger of being destroyed by ideas and values alien to the ones with which they grew up, find the transition bewildering, if not intolerable, and seek refuge by keeping themselves to themselves. It's hardly surprising they sometimes give the impression of wanting to keep outsiders, now decidedly insiders, out.

Get to know them, and you quickly realize they are neither aloof nor standoffish, the very opposite. But in the meantime, their reputation for being suspicious of strangers, including those of us who settle in the village, is likely to continue, suggesting divisions between the old and the new which in fact don't exist more than superficially.

There is, however, one distinction that remains, ineradicable and obvious at second glance – the distinction between the authentic countryman and the ex-townee. If we newcomers live here for another half century I doubt whether our background will cease to confirm that countrymen are born not made. To move to the country is one thing, to become a countryman is something else. As soon as I'm tempted to think otherwise, I meet a true rustic to expose the unbridgeable gulf between us.

A case in point is a man I've met at farm sales, sales I attend not primarily to buy anything but to enjoy the festive atmosphere, one, incidentally, that often strikes me as contradictory, bearing in mind the frequently sad reason behind the disposal. He looks to be in his seventies, paradoxically stands out by being so short of stature, and has a face either weather-beaten, too hurriedly washed, or permanently in need of a shave. His emaciated body appears held together by its threadbare garments; a red woollen headpiece worn in all weathers envelops his ears and almost covers his nearly shoulder-length hair. He is, stretching politeness to its limit, the embodiment of scruffiness.

Yet his eyes, mischievous, impish, darting everywhere not to miss a trick, convey he hasn't a care in the world. Or respect for anybody that isn't earned.

Many a time I've watched him bid without opening his mouth; the merest eye movement communicates he's still in the hunt. Until I came to know him better, I used to wonder what in the world he did with all the bits and pieces he accumulated, an unlikely conglomeration if ever there was one. Soon I realized he didn't give the stuff away!

I was queuing behind him at the auctioneer's receipt of custom to pay for a rare purchase I'd made of horse brasses, once used to enhance the appearance of harness on shires but now decorating the fireplace of our cottage. The back of his hand was bleeding profusely. He ignored it apart from periodically wiping it on his trousers.

Just before his turn to pay he started to scratch under his left arm, as though fighting off an invasion of fleas; almost tied himself up in a knot.

Then I understood! He was simply trying to reach into a pocket in that unlikely region. Out came a wad of notes as thick as your arm, mostly fives and tens. Aware he was now the focal point of attention, he nonchalantly counted the sum required, handed it over like a man with no arms, and restored the remainder to his armpit vault. His leathery face never stopped smiling.

My next encounter with the armpit bank astonished me by a totally different side to his character, indicating, I'm happy to admit, we had more in common than unshaven faces.

At a barn dance!

You wouldn't believe with what abandon he defied his years, dragging shrinking violets far younger than himself into the fray, the life and soul of the party as the night proceeded.

Dancing for him was more a way of life, only *barn* dancing, mark you, not what this normally taciturn man called modern disco nonsense.

Some days later, chatting with another old countryman

and his wife, I soon gathered that barn dances sometimes mark the beginning of life-long partnerships. As we sat drinking tea in their farmhouse they reminisced . . .

She was sixteen, winsomely unsure of herself, more at ease driving a tractor than dancing a hoedown. He, a year older, responded to her emerging womanhood as befitted a man of the world.

Their love grew like a sun-drenched harvest – imperceptible, ripening, golden. And before the winter wheat was sown they were planning to get married, planning naturally with well ploughed country caution – when he'd served his time in the village butcher's shop, when she wasn't quite so indispensable on her father's one-man farm, when they'd saved enough for down payment on a small-holding, when . . .

They hoped. And dreamed. And waited. He became a master butcher; she toiled on the farm, increasingly in the farmhouse as her mother's health began seriously to fail. Within months the sick woman was incapable of doing anything for herself, wholly dependent on her only daughter.

Six years of unrelieved suffering later, lovingly cared for at home to the last, she died peacefully in her sleep, a relief even the grieving family could not begrudge.

'Wipe your tears, lass,' her father told her, 'arrange the date of your wedding. It's what Mother would want. You've waited too long already. Much too long.'

But before she had a mind to give herself to such happiness, her father too, in what proved to be his own long last illness, urgently required the same ungrudging care lavished upon his wife.

His protests that the wedding should go ahead anyway fell on deaf ears. 'I want *you* to give me away,' she encouraged him. So while his married son, himself a farmer, kept an eye on the family farm, she remained fully occupied in the farmhouse.

Meanwhile the man impatient to make her his wife, seeing she was adamant that either to leave her sick father or remain to care for him was no way to start a marriage, agreed there was nothing else in the circumstances they could do, nothing at all.

But wait.

The wedding took place shortly after her thirty-first birthday, the recently tolling church bells going crazy in celebration as she and the master butcher walked from the church man and wife at last. Many of the older villagers, having grown up with her mother and father, were in tears, doubtless mindful of why the happy day was so belated.

The newly-weds were fortunate to find a cottage with a bit of land, and sank the rest of their savings in a few hens and a housecow. Before rushing off to work, he milked it at first light, and repeated the exercise before sitting down to supper.

She made butter and cheese, added to the hens, and developed a vegetable garden, selling at the door everything surplus to their own requirements, with one purpose in mind.

To *buy* a farm of their own was, they realized, out of the question, but to *rent* one might be possible; a small farm, big enough, though, they carefully calculated, to provide a living for the pair of them working side by side.

Yet when an early chance came unexpectedly he hesitated. Argued. Worried their income without his regular wages as a master butcher would be precarious, an invitation to debt, something he couldn't abide.

'We must!' she tenderly silenced his fears.

Working all hours of the day and half the night, he

78

concentrated on improving their only guaranteed income, a monthly cheque for the milk from at first four, then six, and finally ten Friesians.

She brought all her experience of growing up on a farm to their tiny flock – trimming hoofs, clipping backsides, douching, inspecting for footrot, dipping, and – highlight of her year for as far back as she could remember – the lambing.

As a child she'd watched and subsequently helped her dad too often with ewe or teg in trouble not to know almost by instinct what to do. And she loved every minute as much now as in those far off days, despite the occasional still-born or lambs dying within minutes or days of birth.

The advent of new life never failed to excite her, give her a sense of achievement, specially when she bottle fed orphans, some too weak to stand, cradled in her arms, tugging at her own maternal longings. Watching twins and triplets growing sturdy, soon indistinguishable from the biggest single lambs as they all raced and frolicked, bursting with energy, celebrating for her the arrival of spring, she felt profound contentment, somehow lifted above the inescapable weariness.

The day things began to go wrong – or right, who knows? – dawned like any other. He'd already done the milking and was back for breakfast.

The phone rang. A voice neither of them knew arranged a meeting at the farm for later that day, no doubting the urgency.

She prepared cups and saucers, and minutes before the visitor was due put the kettle on; her husband moved to the door as the car arrived. She handed a cup to the man in a pin-stripe suit, answering his enquiry that holidays were out of the question – who'd feed the animals, do the milking? – though she and her husband did occasionally find time to visit the airfield on the boundary of the next village to watch members of a parachute club practising their sport, something she often thought she'd like to try herself.

'We've a good life here,' she summed up.

Her husband nodded. Smiled. 'Hard, though,' his eyes twinkled. She searched his face. 'The opposite of exciting,' he teased.

The pin-stripe suit looked from one to the other, unsure they weren't sharing a private joke, and attempting to spoon the rest of his sodden biscuit from the saucer.

He reached for his briefcase, and cleared his throat, suddenly serious. The fact of the matter was, he dropped his bombshell, the farm was to be put up for sale. As sitting tenants they had the first option. Otherwise they'd have to move. The asking price, fair enough, even considerate, sounded to them like a sick joke.

To borrow so much from the bank would take forever to repay, and – they saw in a flash – surely turn the rest of their lives into something like running up an escalator coming down. Was it worth it? Or really feasible?

The man picked up his bowler hat. 'I'll need to know within three days,' he announced. 'Give me a ring.'

And he was gone.

The thought of starting all over again! Just when this place was beginning encouragingly to pay its way – and feel as secure and snug as their childhood homes. She stared at her husband, saw the disappointment in his eyes, and felt empty of comfort.

'I want to stay,' he tried to be cheerful; 'we both do, I know. But the thought of all that debt!' He dropped his voice. 'And suppose you have a baby . . .' His wretchedness made their dearest hope sound dreadful.

'We'll manage,' she struggled to overcome her doubts. 'Somehow.'

'We can't stay,' he was definite. 'Be a millstone round our necks. You know it will. We'll have to move.'

She seemed far away, barely conscious of his agitation. Slowly her face eased into brightness, and she clapped her hands like a child again riding on top of the hay wagon.

'What about the hoedown?' she said.

He looked puzzled.

'You remember! Our first barn dance. You kept saying the only way to enjoy ourselves was to put a firm foot forward and try not harder but easier. Remember! Well?' she positioned herself ready to start the dance.

They glided round the kitchen table, into the lounge, out again, sometimes falling over each other's feet, all the time hardly able to sing the tune for laughing.

'I think,' he imitated the voice of the man in the pin-stripe suit, 'I think *you* ought to stay and if you're staying, I'm staying too. I didn't wait all that time to marry you . . . to live on my own.'

They glided round the kitchen table once more before he disappeared to do the milking. She returned to sorting her seed potatoes. Both of them still inwardly dancing the hoedown.

The above is, of course, my attempt to recapture the *spirit* of their telling, an afternoon I shan't forget in a hurry for its essential simplicity and so much more I can't begin to depict; altogether wholesome and somehow a celebration.

And there was a postscript!

Years after the pin-stripe suit was forgotten, another important visitor was awaited. As before, this time poking fun at herself for her aches and pains as she poured the tea, she handed a cup to him as soon as he arrived, invited him to help himself from a large tin of biscuits, and settled in a wheelchair, grateful to take the weight off her legs since falling heavily over a hose pipe in the vegetable garden.

He fumbled among his papers, cleared his throat but changed his mind about delivering the little speech he'd surely prepared, and ceremoniously handed over the deeds of the farm.

The three of them couldn't stop laughing, the man from the bank, knowing all they'd achieved, genuinely delighted for them. She was lost for words. Her husband was surprised to find himself eager to recall all the years of scrimping and saving, struggling to make ends meet, attempting what, even at the best of times, his pessimism feared was beyond them.

'We've done it,' he chuckled, 'just the two of us. We've done it!'

And unashamedly he felt proud of himself. Proud.

All she could think about was, she said, their first barn dance at the village hall. How he'd taught her to try not harder but easier.

'There's only one thing that bothers us now,' she told me when next I saw them. Her husband shuffled uneasily. We'd just come in from my meeting their remaining solitary Friesian, providing more than enough for the old couple's needs from one milking a day. 'What would happen,' she searched for words, 'I mean, if anything happened to one of us? We couldn't manage alone, either of us.' She paused. 'We weren't blessed with children, you see,' she whispered.

'We'd finish up in one of those . . . one of those institutions,' he finally managed to spit out the dreaded word.

'Did he show you the sheep?' She changed the subject

abruptly. 'Last year we had eight more, but they all died, some infection, the vet said.'

'We've still got six,' he sounded philosophical, 'more than enough for us at our time of life.'

She pointed to his eightieth birthday cards lingering on the mantelpiece, merrily making the point she herself was soon to reach this milestone. 'It's hard to believe where all the years have gone,' she sighed, not mournfully, rather like someone wishing she could start again – another village hall barn dance as a sixteen-year-old. 'But you can't put the clock back,' she said; 'there's a lot of peace wrapped up in the parcel of acceptance.'

Was this, I wondered as I came away, another bit of country wisdom? I'd never heard the saying before, or since, for that matter, but it summed up so much of the outlook or attitude of some of the characters I was getting to know. Their acceptance was the opposite of submission or begrudging resignation. I can't be sure whether it was helped by their never having been, or wanting to be, part of the rat race; or simply their capacity for differentiating between what could or could not be changed.

But the way they coped in situations they would never in a million years have chosen for themselves, gave the impression that living in the country of itself guaranteed peace of mind; a false impression, of course. Such serenity was by no means universal among us.

7

Mating squirrels and the horse midwife

One day I almost literally stumbled across a man as he rebuilt a hedge, a skill made to look deceptively easy by a true craftsman. Using his hook, bill-hook or slasher, he worked his way from one end of the field to the other, cutting back, thinning out, reinforcing, encouraging growth, making it all seem so simple, well within the ability of even the hamfisted like me. It isn't. I have the scars to prove it.

This craftsman didn't mind working and talking at the same time, so I felt encouraged to ask him about something I'd seen in the woods, something puzzling going back to my days at school, rooted deeply enough to continue to challenge the evidence of my own eyes.

Our natural history teacher, Miss Spring, only appeared fierce because her massive bun gave the impression she had two heads, a likely character for some of the gentle fairy stories to which she also felt constrained to introduce us.

Her method of transferring information or learning from her mind to ours can be summed up in one word. Repetition. She told us. We repeated the enlightenment. And so on ad infinitum. The result was that I, never mind the other thirty-nine or so innocents, left her zealous care knowing everything and understanding nothing.

Squirrels were a typical illustration. Miss Spring told us they hibernated. I at least repeated this truism with the same understanding that hedgehogs and dormice hibernated. They all retired for the winter, slept in their snug havens as protection from both severe weather and the absence of food. Proof was the way squirrels collected nuts and buried them to ensure a ready supply in the early days of their emergence.

It could be argued, of course, that I wasn't very bright; that Miss Spring's teaching was further handicapped by the fact I'd never seen a squirrel, and lacked aspirations in that direction. But she was emphatic about everything, searing in my mind that what she said was *gospel* and unforgettable if repeated often enough.

Which leaves me with the other conclusion, that Miss Spring herself believed squirrels hibernated in exactly the same way as hedgehogs and dormice. And why not? After all, even the great Gilbert White of Selborne suspected at one time if not until he died that swifts and swallows hibernated, based upon his own astute observations and logic. One moment he saw them on the wing, the next they were gone. Either they were flying to warmer climes, thousands of miles away, or curling up for the winter. The first alternative stretched his credulity to breaking point; how could such tiny birds undertake, never mind survive, such a journey both ways?

We are all the children of our age!

So if Miss Spring believed squirrels hibernated like hedgehogs and dormice, who was I to question this morsel of knowledge as I journeyed into adulthood increasingly surrounded by concrete, not a squirrel in sight! From such acorns of misinformation or misunderstanding in childhood do mighty oaks of ignorance grow.

The first hint that my particular oak was grossly malformed was on a November morning in the woods, far too nippy for any self-regarding squirrel to be about. Yet I spotted one. It shot up a tree, to the far side out of sight, and was gone, to where I couldn't make out, despite taking my time to look carefully: no apparent holes, not a drey in sight.

I might have been tempted to suspect an optical illusion but for a second sighting that same afternoon, and another a whole three weeks or so later. Astonished, I reconciled these *phenomena* with my belief about squirrels and hibernation by rationalizing that the weather wasn't all that cold, not in our milder south-eastern climate. Perhaps our privileged squirrels retired to their winter quarters rather later.

This was, however, before a bleak early afternoon in January, wind howling, snow flakes whirling, the temperature low enough to persuade even the boldest of brass monkeys to remain indoors. The squirrel was bouncy, scurrying between trees, stopping only to cast a glance in my direction before shooting up one, again to disappear without trace. But what finally persuaded me that Miss Spring had herself somehow got it wrong or failed to penetrate my understanding with the whole truth about squirrels in winter, was the one I spotted when the snow was inches deep, much of it frozen solid.

Well, having related these essential facts to the craftsman working at the hedge, I asked the inevitable question. They do *not* hibernate, he was emphatic, but leave their dreys usually only on warmer days; surprised you saw one on a bitterly cold afternoon. He paused, though not from his work. Bloody pests they are, his vehemence surprised me, play havoc with young trees and birds' eggs; we call 'em vermin. Tree rats.

There was another aspect of squirrel behaviour that puzzled me, something I observed when the sap was rising in apparently more ways than one. Alone in the woods, absorbed into the stillness to listen and watch, I heard a distant disturbance in the trees. In no time at all a squirrel shot past, too preoccupied to notice me, followed by half-a-dozen or so other squirrels seemingly in hot pursuit, likewise too single-minded to bother about me. A game of hide 'n' seek? Or war? Either appeared possible. It was all over in a flash, and an hour later I left the woods still wondering.

If I could have found the hedge builder I would have asked him, but after perhaps three weeks of working from one end of the field to the other, the job completed, he'd disappeared, and I hadn't seen him since.

So – I didn't exactly forget about it through lack of interest; but with spring giving way to summer I found myself thinking about other things, many of them equally fascinating.

I was reminded about the incident by the retired shepherd complaining about the damage squirrels were reputed to be doing in some village gardens; invading bird tables, he said, plundering nests and even taking fledglings.

What did *he* think about my observation in the woods?

'When was this?' he asked, his heavily ploughed face wreathed in smiles.

'The beginning of May,' I quickly calculated.

'Randy little buggers,' he said, 'they were playing all right, but it was more than a game to them; the oldest game of all,' he laughed. 'Mating!'

He went on to explain that as many as a dozen males – possibly more! – sometimes chased a solitary female, each and every one of them fiendishly single-minded about the exclusive prize. And the reward was not necessarily granted to the first in the chase! Not on your life, he claimed. This favour was the prerogative of the female herself, though how or why she discriminated he wisely claimed not to know. One thing's for sure, he summed up, apart from the squirrel granted the prize, the chasing group needed to look elsewhere for their gratification.

Mumbling *ain't nature wonderful* to my wife, I told her about this peculiar style of copulation. 'Never mind about *that*,' she sounded agitated, 'have you heard about the village odd-job man?'

We first met him within days of our arrival, outside the village post office. He looked in his late twenties, was almost as short as he was round, and had bushy hair resting not only on his shoulders but peering massively from his open shirt. Despite his abundant waistline, his trousers were much too big, giving the suggestion he was likely to fall straight through at any moment, disappear altogether. But the legs were too short, well above the ankles, and tapered to look not unlike jodhpurs. Their frayed bottoms were partly covered by the lining of his overcoat which – we were soon to realize – he wore in all weathers.

Definitely what you might call an individual style.

As I climbed from the car he ran towards me, his face beaming, uninhibited, like a sunrise at the height of summer.

'Hello, hello,' he said, pushing out his hand to test the joints of mine in greeting. 'I'm pleased to meet you, pleased to meet you.'

He seemed a compulsive repeater, and this gave the paradoxical impression he didn't have enough words to express his friendliness. Momentarily I felt rather embarrassed and overwhelmed, as though I'd been taken over by a mind empty of reason.

It didn't take me long, of course, to discover that this simple effusive man talked to everybody, but *everybody*, often barging in unwanted, detaining people beyond their wishes, and following them still muttering his repetitions, for twenty steps or so as they made good their escape. Yet once his ways were accepted, his cheerful greeting and handshake brightened many a day.

Incapable of looking after himself, he lived with his grandmother, just the two of them, in a cottage, one up and down, the only home she'd known in her eighty-one years. By repute she was a perfect neighbour, kindness itself to everybody. Specially her grandson, the apple of her eye.

Their symbiotic relationship was mutually rewarding. Her arthritic immobility made her virtually as dependent upon him as his limited understanding upon her. Which perhaps explained why they gave the impression of total contentment with their lot, a lot hardly likely to evoke envy from the most impoverished.

He was, as I say, the odd-job man – cutting lawns, helping with gardening, picking fruit, standing at the foot of a ladder, lifting and carrying, exercising dogs, even assisting with the painting of the outside of a house. No opportunity was lost, the assumption being he would, time and time again, be shown what was required; but once he understood there was no doubting either his application or dependability. I noticed him doing some outside painting, and was both surprised and impressed. No question, he did a good job. Left to his own speed he plodded on regardless of time, the weather, and pretty well everything else, apart from people. Whatever or wherever his employment, he seemed incapable of not breaking off to offer his characteristic greeting, undeterred by responses that sometimes only feebly reflected his own enthusiasm.

I've no idea how he managed for money. He wasn't paid 'proper' wages, though why not always struck me as unfair, for within his limitations he did as good a job as many a person in regular employment. Half the trouble was, I imagine, he didn't expect to be paid in any other way. People gave him tips, amounts he no more refused than questioned. Much or little, he appeared equally satisfied.

Sad to relate, it was this bit of pocket money – for that's all it was – that landed him in the nasty situation behind my wife's agitation. Nothing, you see, appeared to give him greater pleasure than to fill his pocket with sweets, and hand some to every child he met. Knowing him, most of them eagerly accepted; a few never overcame either their shyness or parental warnings about not talking to strangers, both perfectly understandable. Indeed, until getting to know this harmless man myself, I too was inclined to believe that the mentally handicapped were capable of all manner of weird behaviour, some of it embarrassing or frightening because of its unpredictability. So much, I admit, for the prejudice of my ignorance.

Anyhow, this generosity with sweets underlines just how easily misunderstandings of such a nature can occur. It happened so innocently. He was near the village green, waiting as usual for the children's home-going time from school. A couple of little girls ran to the swings and began to heave themselves higher and higher.

They ignored his greeting.

He tried to put sweets in their hands.

One child screamed. The other joined in.

Their parents, holiday-makers passing through, came running.

One look was enough. The father waded in, knocking the supposed molester to the ground. Only the fortuitous arrival of the village policeman prevented more serious damage. He bundled the bewildered odd-job man into a police car, and drove him home, trying to explain!

I continued to see this victim of his own generosity almost every time I went to the village. He still managed somehow not to fall through his trousers, beamed benevolence on the world in general, and found plenty of opportunities to hire out his limited talents – a man as guileless as he was cheerful. Possibly his insensitivity in seeking to monopolize everybody he met caused a degree of irritation if not occasionally downright resentment, but I wasn't the only one by a vast majority in the village who found his simple openness winsome.

Then he appeared to have disappeared!

I inquired in the village shop.

'Haven't you heard! He's gone; taken away.'

'Not that nonsense again!' I recalled his trouble with the sweets.

'No, nothing like that.' The woman behind the counter was clearly put out.

'What about his grandmother?' I asked.

'Oh, didn't you know! She's dead.'

And I listened to a sad tale. It seems he'd arrived home at the usual time, to find his grandmother asleep in her chair. Most strange. Normally she would have had his dinner on the table. When he couldn't wake her, he'd told the woman next door who'd phoned for the village policeman.

With no one to look after him, the odd-job man had been sent to a hostel of some sort miles away, while more permanent arrangements could be made. Little chance, apparently, of his ever returning to our village to live.

And so it has proved. We haven't set eyes on him since. What in the world *he* makes of it all I can't imagine.

Not surprisingly this was one of the first topics of conversation when next I met the retired shepherd; but as is the way with unhappy exchanges that don't become obsessions we moved on to other things, among them the village wedding we'd both helped to celebrate.

'Lovely girl,' he said, 'such a pity she's had to move away. We lose all our youngsters,' he lamented, 'but what else can they do!'

It was, however, my reference to how charmed my wife and I had been by the horse and carriage and the flowing beard in the Victorian coachman's uniform that really brought our chatting alive.

'You know about Dolly?' he referred to the horse.

And seeing my reaction this man full of lambing tales needed no encouragement to put me wise.

This time of the year, he began, Dolly keeps her eyes open. As soon as she spots ewe or teg moving away from the flock, then pawing the ground, turning in its own length, lying down, getting up, pawing a bit more, and finally settling, the usual preliminaries to lambing, she strolls across, not too near, mark you, just enough to be in touch with proceedings.

Soon after the lamb drops, Dolly moves in and helps to lick it clean. Happens time after time. Funny old business. Never known anything like it before. And the sheep don't appear to mind. They naturally lick as well, but make no attempt to exclude Dolly. A sheep can be fiercely protective of its lamb, take it from me, he said. I've seen 'em see off a sheepdog.

This story of Dolly led to a discussion of how horses had been replaced by tractors, more's the pity, the retired shepherd muttered; but not entirely replaced at a farm, he said, between our village and the next.

'When you're in that area,' he told me, 'pop in and tell the farmer I sent you. He'll be pleased to show you his horses.'

The idea appealed, but – by no means persuaded a complete stranger would be all that welcome – I forgot about it, caught up, in any case, if not by lambing itself, at least by legions of lambs, gambolling just beyond our garden gate.

Few sights are more delightful in the country, I reckon, than lambs at play – springing straight up on all fours, dancing, cavorting, racing in groups for the sheer pleasure of nothing more than apparently their own existence. A picture of irrepressible exuberance and celebration!

They don't appear to notice the tight elastic band round the tail to dock it, and also round the testicles to achieve what all the farmers and shepherds I know unanimously believe to be a painless form of castration.

These elastic bands are fitted with an instrument simple to operate, and their effectiveness soon becomes evident as tails litter the pasture. I recall picking up my first three or four, examining them with childlike excitement, and taking them home to show my wife. She seemed less than enthusiastic; and now, scores of lambs' tails later, my own reaction reflects hers. But the antics of the lambs themselves continue to charm, though charm is doubtless not the way everybody sees it.

I recall first watching twin lambs suckling, one either side of their mobile dairy. The manner in which they each plugged themselves on to a teat reminded me of an old film I once saw of a Chicago tough guy biting off the end of a cigar! The twins appeared to be not so much searching for the teat as burrowing for it; and generally speaking this viciousness develops with their size.

The ewe, excellent mother though she was, tolerated the battering for no more than seconds at a time, sure sign she thought they were only greedy. Then she dismissed her charges by lifting the appropriate hind leg over their heads, leaving them open mouthed as she moved away. Time after time, as determined as they.

Equally amusing were lambs chasing rabbits! On reflection maybe chasing is too strong, but that's certainly what it looked like, for minutes at a stretch. Each time the lambs approached, the rabbits side-stepped, just a couple of hops, no more, leaving the lambs to shoot past, gaze back seemingly bewildered, and start the futile exercise all over again. It happened repeatedly, the whole operation finally giving the impression of being mechanically controlled.

In the end, presumably exasperated, the lambs lowered their heads and charged. Once more the rabbits hopped aside, sat upright as though adopting a posture of superiority, and waited for the next episode of fun. But was it, I couldn't help but wonder, really a game or something akin to pecking order aggression?

I'm constantly amazed how wild animals, predator and potential victim alike, react or adjust to each other. Half a dozen rabbits indifferently watching a fox trotting nearby! Do they instinctively know the vixen is already well fed, too satiated to bother or care about the next meal?

And what about a rabbit chasing a stoat? You don't believe it! Well, neither did I, until my informant insisted he'd seen it with his own eyes. The stoat was doubtless too full from a recent kill to care whether the rabbit was following it or not. As for the rabbit, it knew that a well-fed stoat is – for the time being – a predator without teeth! Perfect opportunity for bravado or a bit of fun?

Of more immediate concern at the time I was watching lambs chasing rabbits was my first encounter with myxomatosis. I'm learning to accept that what we see as cruel is nature's benevolent way of separating the weak from the strong, but this disease was, I have to admit, something else, a bit too much for a greenhorn like me. And to compound my outraged susceptibilities, the infection reputedly orginated in our part of the country, the Garden of England itself, sometime in the mid-1950s!

The one corpse I saw was more than enough. Only one? That's right, for by the time we arrived at Hide 'n' Seek the rabbits were well on their way to proving themselves tougher than the disease, finally reducing its wholesale ravishes to near impotence.

But what, in consequence, are we to do with the hordes of these resilient little creatures which appear to be taking over? Virtually every time I look through our kitchen window I see a dozen or so; on our walks they appear to be everywhere in abundance; last night in the woods they were more numerous than the mosquitoes, which is not unlike saying that the immeasurable is greater than the incalculable.

You see my point! We're being overrun – and I for one unashamedly love it. Some people, I gather, find it helpful to unwind by watching tropical fish. Give me wild rabbits at play anytime.

8

Strays in the wood and non-hunting crackpots?

If lambs going full tilt at rabbits surprised me, I'm not sure how to convey the impact of an experience in the woods shortly afterwards.

It was Saturday morning. I was there before breakfast, still addicted to the music of the trees, trying without much success to distinguish by sound alone one species from another.

Through a fire-break I spotted a couple of horses, riderless, no harness, too full of themselves to be bothered by my presence. They strolled past like contented ramblers.

It didn't take the genius of a Sherlock Holmes to work out they were strays from a neighbouring farm, and I felt a strong obligation to do something about their return. Yes, but what? To catch them was beyond me, a conclusion I gratefully reached after a half-hearted attempt, and in any case I didn't know the farm. Could have been anywhere. All things considered I left them to it.

Some ten minutes later, looking as though he carried at least the burdens of the whole world, a man came into view. And together we set off to round up his horses. Elementary! He slipped halters over their heads – cooperation from one, plenty of tossing from the other – and turned his face homeward.

Did I ride? he asked. I admitted I didn't. You don't follow the hounds, then! He quickly put two and two together. Inexplicably my silent agreement prompted him to cast a sly look of condemnation in my direction, as though he'd found me out secretly committing the unspeakable. I hope, he said, you're not one of them crackpots who oppose blood sports.

To be honest, I wasn't sure, not at the time. I thought I was a crackpot, but living in the country was, as it were, testing my prejudgements. No doubt about my ideas shifting. The day before, I'd met a wood-cutter and his mate thinning a spinney, and also incidentally grumbling like mad the place hadn't been touched for years. It's like working in a coal mine, they'd said; some afternoons we leave when it's dark, but once away from the trees discover the sun's still shining.

What persuaded me I was, more to the point, changing fundamentally in my ideas and outlook was my reaction to the wood-cutter's excitement in describing how he'd seen a kestrel take a blue-tit in flight. Whoosh! All over in a moment. 'It was beautiful,' he said. 'Beautiful.'

And I understood perfectly what he meant! Not so long before I would have been horrified, outraged. Now I appreciated how and why this life-long wood-cutter soon to retire remained little short of awestruck at such a sight.

It reminded me of watching, heart in my mouth, a fox take a rabbit. I was mesmerized, almost afraid to look, too identified with the rabbit to enjoy the skill of the fox. Or so I thought! In the event, I followed every movement with growing admiration, still inwardly cringing at the outcome, yet not doubting for a moment that this was nature's way and in its own setting, to use the wood-cutter's surprising word, beautiful.

So the man leading his two horses from the woods might have been right in calling me, or implying I was, a crackpot, but I honestly didn't know. And a fortnight or so later I was even less sure, having experienced the serendipity of two red-coated huntsmen, just the two, with a full pack of hounds, tearing along the side of my favourite woods in pursuit, I gathered from one of the handful of followers on foot, of a couple of foxes.

One huntsman galloped round to the other side of the part of the woods jutting out to the boundary of a field of kale, hoping to cut off at least one of the intended victims as the dogs closed in, but what in fact happened was surely the biggest anti-climax of hunting history. In a word – nothing. But that's the whole point. This exercise in futility was simply charming to watch, like a Christmas card come alive. The huntsmen didn't appear to mind they'd been given the slip; the hounds, tongues elongated, yapped with weary delight from the chase; the followers on foot, myself now among them, could hardly have looked less bloodthirsty; and eventually we all dispersed with renewed respect for Reynard.

Of course, it could have ended differently, as we shall see.

But I hope you can also see how my interest in horses was imperceptibly growing!

This momentum was quickened innocuously enough by a picture postcard from a city acquaintance with printer's ink in her veins. I read her delightful greeting and turned to the other side: two shire horses, controlled by a traditional countryman who could have been my old cottager, pulling an ancient seed driller, watched by two other shires, the quartet simply magnificent.

I pinned the card up in our kitchen; and at the first opportunity inquired of my cottager friend, fund of all local knowledge, gossip and scandal, if anybody in the neighbourhood owned shire horses.

He was categoric. No! Didn't I realize, he went on – went on in more ways than one! – that a horse and man could plough no more than an acre a day, whereas a small tractor could manage at least twenty-five? When he was a lad the countryside was full of horses, but since the mid-1930s, he reckoned, they'd given way to tractors until now it was like looking for a needle in a haystack to find one. And they call it progress! He almost spat the words in my eye.

My wife was characteristically pragmatic. If I was so interested, she suggested, what about a visit to Regent's Park on Easter Monday – for the annual horse show? There were bound to be lots of shires pulling brewery wagons if nothing else. A day back in the old haunts should be fun!

And, of course, she was right, at least about the shires. Teams of six and eight in pairs, controlled by unashamedly proud, bowler hatted, immaculately uniformed handlers, bringing to our attention that some brew or other was better or darker or whatever. Without exception every handler was an enthusiast, apparently living for little else, as one wife half laughingly confirmed, the lot of them never happier than when talking among themselves about their job or to anyone else genuinely interested.

By the time we turned homeward I was hooked. There's no need, my wife kept repeating, to go over the top. And she was right, of course; no need at all. The fact that my life could never be quite the same again was coincidental.

Now I've often wondered whether our predominant ideas, anxieties, fears, interests, act as a sort of magnet, attracting to ourselves the very things, joys or calamities, we can't stop thinking or worrying about. I met a person shortly after moving here who confidently lived on the assumption or expectation that something or other was bound to go wrong, just round the corner, and was so often proved right.

More personally, I've noticed that if I come across a new word or idea or name, I meet it all over the place during the next few days; inescapable. Coincidence? Probably, though I prefer to remain agnostic. Anyhow, let me tell you what happened shortly after our return from the Regent's Park horse parade.

One of our nearer neighbours was – and I resist the temptation to name drop – a TV comedian, very good, too, spontaneously funny even *off* the screen. He and his teenage son farmed a few acres at the back of our cottage, farmed them as efficiently as lovingly. It was an education for my wife and me to watch how much, without resorting to intensive farming, they were able to work their limited acreage.

Trouble was, apart from another field they managed to rent from the parish council, their hope of expansion was nil, with bigger farms closing in, getting ever bigger and bigger. The comedian and his son knew their tiny farm wasn't financially viable, and never could be, not the way they both wanted, which, apart from anything else, explained why the older man remained an entertainer with diminishing enthusiasm. His dearest wish was to farm full-time.

Our feelings were mixed, I can tell you, the morning we wished him and his family farewell, sad to lose such superb neighbours, happy they had the chance to move to a hundred-plus acres in Wales. The new tenants, they told us, planned to arrive within a few days.

We didn't see or hear them. Whoever or whatever they were, they were quiet. One day the farmhouse and outbuildings were empty, the next mid-morning fully occupied, the latter, as far as we could see, with calves. Over the next few days we heard the tractor, no real indication of what it was doing. To tell you the truth, I began to wonder whether they'd brought any more stock with them at all, so devoid of farm activity had the place become.

Then a couple of cattle transporters and a large horse-box arrived, once more, in terms of noise, followed by near silence. Most peculiar, not to say tantalizing.

I caught my first sight of the shire horses some five days later, a pair of them being led into a field for the day. The person leading them immediately reminded me of the character on my picture postcard – slightly rotund, stocky, jacket without sleeves, and a face that looked as though he'd just won the pools.

He told me his interest in horses originated in his sister's pony, a gift from their parents, and his happiness in sharing its care. Then his father, a general trader, bought a horse and cart, not a shire but a sturdy stallion, and increasingly allowed his son to take the reins.

After this, as the son himself said, one thing led to another, in his case a passion, nothing less, to own not only a horse himself but a shire, though why a shire he still could not explain thirty-odd years later. It simply had to be a shire, despite the price, for even in those days such horses weren't cheap, and to a lad struggling to save enough they cost the earth. He was, in fact, well into his twenties before his goal became feasible.

He heard of a shire for sale at a farm near Biddenden, not all that far from here, but miles from his home at the time. No matter, he made the journey, and bartered far far less than he would now before counting out the fortune required – £127.10s, every penny earned and saved by himself over the years. Even as he told me about that milestone in his life his face conveyed how much he was re-living the magic of that first purchase. A dream come true. A shire of his own at last.

The pair of shires he was leading when I first spotted him were a Clydesdale filly and gelding. Once released they pranced with the excitement of children let out of school, kicking their hind quarters, tearing after each other, repeatedly whinnying in celebration, a picture of ecstasy. Their owner beamed his affection and pride.

'Come and see the others.' He led the way to a spacious outbuilding in the farmyard. In separate adjacent sections were a Percheron filly and a Clydesdale stallion of enormous proportions, both magnificent, the latter an immediate eye-catcher because of his sheer bulk.

'Don't you let the four out together?' I inquired, underscoring my ignorance, to be told the stallion was sometimes inclined to rough up the fillies and indeed the gelding.

'Funny thing is,' he continued, anxious to correct any suggestion of implied criticism of his stallion, 'when I take him to shows or exhibitions he behaves like a lamb.' And to prove this herculean gentleness, his owner added: 'I can trust him with children; he lets them lead him into the ring, no danger at all. Lovely temperament. He only gets a bit above himself when the fillies are in season!'

Having felt the weight of the harness kept for shows and the like, I wasn't surprised to learn that the shires themselves weighed at least three-quarters of a ton, every ounce requiring to be perfectly co-ordinated for walking, trotting, and much else I don't pretend to understand – yet! – if an acceptable horse was to become a prize winner.

One thing I did pick up straightaway. Preparation of a concentrated kind for a show or charity performance, the latter increasingly popular these days, started some three months before the event. First thing for fastidious attention was the shoeing, to ensure that by precisely the right time there was no under- or overlapping of the hoofs, no cracks or crevices, nothing to mar an immaculately polished surface.

Next came beauty-queen care of the feathers, hair on the lower part of the legs, ideally, from the judge's standpoint, pure white, a scorer of points, facilitating, I gathered, a degree of ingenuity by the wily; nothing dishonest, you understand, just a little encouragement in the right direction.

Fundamental to the whole preparation period was, of course, the daily routine, which made severe demands of the handler(s) whose commitment, unless motivated by genuine affection and belief in the goal, turned the drudgery, ever daily longer and longer as the date approached, into a nightmare, finally unacceptable.

'You won't find time-servers working with heavy horses,' our new neighbour informed me, re-echoing what I'd been told at Regent's Park: 'Before a show, at least one night before, you can forget your bed.'

Reminiscences plus endless facts about shire horses poured from this enthusiast's lips, and I was delighted to try to cope with the lot. But it wasn't easy, not least because he too quickly changed the subject, dragging me off to inspect the other love of his life.

I gazed in wonderment.

You must have gathered, I've met since coming here all sorts of craftsmen – turning a piece of chestnut into palings or hazel into a hurdle; saving a wood by thinning it; building hedges; working a digger and cutter with the precision of a surgeon's knife; delivering a lamb with a bloated head, no veterinary training apart from a near life-time of shepherding; carving a crook from the horn of a ram; shearing a sheep in little more than a minute, the whole fleece in a single piece; hammering red hot metal into exquisite designs. The catalogue could go on and on.

Now here was something else – an ancient farm wagon recently renovated to look as new, every detail authentic. I didn't need to be told the work had taken years rather than months, a labour of love at every spare moment.

No wonder this particular craftsman rising forty was still a bachelor!

Another aspect of our move to the country reminds me that countrymen are born not made.

Visitors to our new home from the city included an eight-year-old afflicted with what is crudely called in an adult world surplus energy. Nothing a good long walk, I concluded, couldn't cure, a walk crammed with the wonders of natural history. The pair of us set off together, he no less enthusiastic than I.

We climbed a gate, almost immediately spotted a legion of rabbits, to him a novelty, and arrived in a field riddled with mole hills. He was fascinated. We found a discarded stake in the hedge, poking around until the mole's channel was sufficiently clear for him both to see and feel it with his fingers. He couldn't believe it!

Gratified at this early degree of interest, I chatted about an old-fashioned mole plough I'd recently helped to operate, to assist drainage on a nearby farm actually to compensate for the *absence* of moles. Asking what pulled the plough, he perked up no end to hear it was a tractor. 'When I grow up,' he said, 'I'm going to drive a tractor. Well, a tank. There's not all that difference!'

I might have been tempted to query his confidence but we stumbled across a dead chicken, a Rhode Island Red, our eyes attracted in that direction by a magpie, as much detested in the country as crows – unfairly, I think! – already assisting Nature's great re-cycling process.

Who owned the chicken? he wanted to know. What killed it? How did it die? And what was it doing in the middle of a field, a considerable distance from the nearest farmyard? Meanwhile, the magpie continued to stab away at the corpse until we were remarkably close, another source of delight for my young innocent.

You can imagine – we talked about the re-cycling: nothing wasted, death sustaining life; and I threw in the story of the chaffinch. He appeared charmed. Hooked. Already a budding naturalist. Doubtless this one walk in the Garden of England was going to make a permanent impact. No knowing where it might end.

We joked, climbed stiles and more gates, ambled through fields, counted lambs, picked up a few tails, every second between each new sighting or discovery occupied by my flow of information picked up since moving to Hide 'n' Seek. Did he know that five pairs of barn owls were capable of eating 24,000 rats, mice and other rodents all within a square mile? That a family of weasels eat about 2000 mice and voles a year? That squirrels don't bury nuts only in caches, but singly all over the place, and retrieve them not from memory but by sniffing them out, the ones they manage to find? That after a breeding season there are 10,000,000 wood pigeons, most of them, I pulled his leg, in my favourite woods to which we were heading?

I amazed myself by how much I knew; how much I didn't understand.

And look at this! I pointed, genuinely delighted to be able to display my recently acquired knowledge about cuckoo-spit. As a lad I'd believed it *was* what its name suggested – the spit of a cuckoo; and often wondered why the bird should have acquired such a filthy habit!

I gently spread the foam, and there was the larva of a frog-hopper. Whether in fact it remotely resembles a frog or hops like one depends largely, I reckon, on the sort of imagination you possess!

However, I'm not concerned you should believe or disbelieve any of the above figures and facts. More important is that you should get the *feel* of the occasion – an eight-year-old city lad, reminiscent of myself at his age, being introduced to the marvels of nature, introduced by, it must be admitted, a half-baked naturalist whose limited teaching skills were superseded by nothing more than his own enthusiasm and the implicit belief that once a child was exposed to the wonders of the countryside he was an addict for life.

We plodded on, and seemingly in no time at all were within sight of my prize exhibit, the thing I'd had in mind when setting out, guaranteed to hold him spellbound. I led the way into the woods, and soon, as always, felt a mixture of awe, bewilderment and sadness as I spotted the fallen horse-chestnut tree, roots intact, the hole where they had been remarkably shallow, I thought, for such a specimen, no sign of disease; girth of two feet, height of eighteen strides (my own), presumably simply blown down. Or, as the old cottager suggested, fallen over through old age?

As with the dead Rhode Island Red, this giant was already very much a means of life. A tiny plant appeared to be firmly rooted in a recess of the trunk; innumerable beetles scurried; an animal or animals had already feasted on some of the bark.

What do you think, I called over my shoulder, did it fall or was it pushed? I turned. He was nowhere to be seen. I called his name. Nothing. Retracing my steps I shouted again, louder, also informing him this was no time for games.

My eyes darted, I strained to listen, anxious to discover

his hiding place, enjoying the joke but a little apprehensive. At first I was puzzled by the buzz coming from the other side of a hedge just beyond the boundary of the woods. It sounded as I drew nearer like a motorbike or perhaps a jet on take-off.

He was standing in the front seat of a disintegrating van which looked as though it had been abandoned the day after Mr Ford set his conveyor production moving. What it was doing there, the middle of nowhere, must remain a mystery. Surely not abandoned by the farmer! Yet if not, who would have gone to so much trouble to dump a van?

My budding naturalist was in his seventh heaven, rescued from the wonders all around him by a spaceship called, he solemnly informed me, a Zoid. A what? I asked. A Zoid, he repeated, not hiding his contempt for my obvious ignorance; surely you've heard of a Zoid!

The unearthly noise continued from his lips. He flung himself about, destroying an attacking spacecraft, at the same time making it abundantly clear to me that this scrap-heap heading for Mars was likely to keep him occupied for ever. Finally persuaded, he made a superb landing, clambered out with zealous reluctance, and immediately reprimanded me for not telling him about this Zoid.

I admitted I hadn't seen it before, despite frequent sorties in the region, an admission which caused him, I fear, to view me and my love for the countryside in an entirely new light.

'Come and see this fallen horse-chestnut,' I apologized; and we continued on our now incompatible way, I steering him away from his boredom with the fallen giant to another part of the woods. My belated aim was to salvage something from this débâcle by trying something I'd watched Tony Soper demonstrate a couple days or so

107

before in his TV programme *Discovering Animals*. Guided by an expert in the study of small mammals, he'd simply crept up to a piece of corrugated sheeting lying in a field, gingerly lifted it, and the pair of them had grabbed an assortment of mice and voles.

My wife and I had watched it all, as though we ourselves were there, and even before the programme ended I'd decided to look under a piece of discarded corrugated sheeting in the woods not far from the pens once used for rearing pheasants. Here, surely, was the ideal opportunity.

Right! I said to my young companion, I've something really special to show you. His interest sparked up. Not hanging about, we reached the old pens within minutes, and stood some twenty strides away from the corrugated sheet, incidentally not disturbed, by the look of things, for years. A veritable enticement for every small mammal in the area.

If they hear us, I whispered, they'll be off; we'll see nothing. His co-operation of silence was unnerving. We inched forward. A pin drop would have sounded thunderous. His eyes communicated with mine, inviting commendation for his stealthiness. I smiled encouragingly.

We reached the corrugated sheet. Slowly, ever so slowly, I bent down, tenderly gripped the cover for this collection of small mammals, looked up to be sure my intrepid companion was absolutely ready, and WHOOSH. We both grabbed.

Have you ever wondered what it must feel like to be treated like a skunk inadvertently wandering into a drawing room? Well, from that moment I became an authority on the subject. For two pairs of eyes searched the exposed area for the slightest sign of life – even a solitary wood louse would have been fêted – and seeing nothing one pair turned in my direction, eyes not so much contemptuous as suggesting that skunks in a drawing room were more deserving of tolerance.

Which just goes to show there's more to discovering animals, Mr Soper, than you sometimes make out. As for our eight-year-old city visitor, his subsequent attitude before gratefully leaving the barrenness of the countryside, might have been misinterpreted as meaning I was both an old bore who knew nothing about Zoids and had peculiar ideas about the undersides of discarded corrugated sheets in his favourite woods.

A budding naturalist, if ever there was one!

The same could be said, I was astonished to discover, about at least one bird-watcher we stumbled across whose hide-out fooled us, never mind the birds. We wanted, my wife and I, to rub shoulders with real ornithologists, people who could put us wise about how and where to see a greater variety of species. She phoned the RSPB, and was advised to visit one of their bird sanctuaries, relatively up the road from us.

We went one Saturday morning, early. The kindly warden, in deerstalker hat, binoculars the size of his ample chest, beard as bushy as a cockatoo's tail, received us at the reception office. We were directed to number-one hide. The creaking door heralded our otherwise ignored entry, and we found ourselves in what struck me as being not unlike a holy shrine. The worshippers, shoulder to shoulder, speaking only in reverent whispers, peered through the slit on three sides. Every place was occupied.

We tiptoed to a seat at the back, hoping for a viewing vacancy, meanwhile trying to peer over shoulders. In no time I found myself more fascinated by the bird-watchers than the birds themselves. Such concentration. Excitement. Devoutness. Ecstasy.

'A cormorant,' one of them urgently intoned, 'left of the green island.'

A co-ordinated swing of binoculars focused upon the preening beauty, wholly unconscious of such concerted devotion. Despite our back seats we too would have joined the swing, if we hadn't left to each other the bringing of our prized binoculars. Nevertheless we felt caught up in this act of veneration.

More murmurs of delight. Another co-ordinated swing. This time an oystercatcher, I think, unconsciously receiving the oblations. The atmosphere was electric; quiet, still, but nonetheless electric, full of expectation and hope and a sort of sophisticated wonder, I don't know how else to describe it, for the irreverent thought struck me that some of these evidently vastly experienced ornithologists seemed more concerned to clock up a new sighting than to enjoy the birds themselves.

Eventually, weary of waiting, we moved to the creaking door which alone acknowledged our release, and set off on the sign-posted walk round the sanctuary. Strange, not a bird in sight, not until we came to a flooded worked-out gravel pit splendidly occupied by six ducks, black and white heads, probably coots. Not wasting a moment they took off, leaving us, ornithologically speaking, bereft.

We spread the waterproof. My wife took out a flask of piping hot coffee; and sipping with the satisfaction of aspiring idolaters we too watched enchanted.

Rabbits! And a weasel shooting across the path not a dozen strides away.

Two coffees and a meat pie later, continuing the walk, we stumbled across not a bird but another bird-watcher.

He was stretched out in the midday sun, massive binoculars resting on his chest. Sound asleep.

'We must come again,' I whispered to my wife, 'bird-watching is obviously an acquired art.'

And we tiptoed past, concerned not to disturb our most memorable sighting of the morning.

9

The hunt, two foxes, and a garden full of cats

We were more successful – eventually! – in sighting foxes. And now, make no mistake, I'm no longer entirely a greenhorn in this fascinating area of country life.

Pages back I mentioned that foxes are one of my favourite wild animals, though why, having seen evidence of their devastation in a hen run, is hard to fathom. Half-a-dozen corpses left behind! The carnage, incidentally, prompted a fierce exchange of opinion between the retired shepherd and the owner of the hens.

Understandably in the circumstances the latter hadn't a good word to say for the predator. Left to him every fox in the country would be exterminated, hunting, shooting, any means whatever. But the old shepherd wouldn't have it. According to him – and this surprised me in the light of what a young shepherd had told me only days before – foxes are not wanton killers, slaughtering anything that moves for the sheer fun of it before making off with only one of the victims. He claimed they killed not as plunderers at all, but because their instinct was to go for any prey trying to escape. If only the bloody hens would sit tight, he said, the fox would take just the one, enough for a good meal. The rest would be safe.

You will, I know, appreciate that this proved to be of no comfort at all to the owner of the dead hens. Indeed, he subsequently gave the impression of blaming the retired shepherd for the blood-letting, blaming him on the basis that such an attitude only encouraged the fox!

Nonetheless, despite this latest carnage, plus the

remains of a goose, one of two killed, plus the decidedly ruffled feathers of the young shepherd I mentioned insisting foxes were taking some of his lambs, I wanted to believe this 'enlightened' attitude, wanted to believe it if only because it squared with all I was learning in my own admittedly limited experience of watching foxes.

My admiration if not affection for them remains intact. They are so crafty, up to all manner of dodges if there's remotely anything in it for themselves. But enough of this eulogy. Let me simply try to trace my growing interest in this often less than popular wild creature.

It started really when I spotted my very first fox, totally unexpectedly, in a part of my favourite woods. Saturday afternoon, about three. I must have passed that way a score of times, seeing nothing but squirrels, pheasants, partridges, and naturally plenty of the usual birds.

A disturbance in the undergrowth attracted my attention, and into view came a rabbit running for its life. For a moment I thought I was going to witness the actual kill – at that time a fearful prospect – but the quarry suddenly swerved or dived into a thicket, and the predator appeared tamely to accept defeat; merely stood there, a picture of resignation, making an exhibition of itself for my benefit.

I wasn't concealed, on the contrary, was clearly visible if the fox had slightly turned its head, but it remained perfectly still, ears and brush upright, presumably trying to pick up another scent. And so it remained, for an eternity of perhaps a minute.

My excitement was, I gratefully recall, reminiscent of a childhood Christmas morning. Sheer magic. I stared. The fox stood. Seemingly waiting for me to feast my eyes. Then it meekly trotted away, despite by now being aware of my presence.

After this I didn't see another fox for months. Repeatedly at the same time of the day I returned to the same part of the woods, vigilant, unhurried enough to become absorbed into my surroundings. Nothing. Perhaps, I began seriously to wonder, I hadn't seen a fox at all; stray dog, more likely.

Meanwhile I was getting to know a craftsman maker of palings who worked in the woods well off the beaten track, alone, maybe the reason why he always seemed so pleased to see me. We chatted as he worked, never, as I recall, about foxes. In fact, anything else but foxes.

He would select a piece of chestnut from a pile already cut to size, strip the bark, split the wood once, twice, three and four times, shape the ends, and place the finished pales to make up bundles of twenty. He said he didn't see much wildlife, no doubt because of his chainsaw and the other noisy operations involved in his craft. Another deterrent was his almost constant fire to get rid of the waste wood and strips of bark, a fire necessitated by his legal obligation to keep the woods both tidy and conducive to the trees renewing themselves within ten to twelve years.

But the reputed absence of wildlife in the area of his work wasn't, I suspect, because of either the noise he made or the fire. More likely it was his own preoccupation with maintaining production, a preoccupation amounting to an obsession.

He didn't hurry. Like all the countrymen I knew, he paced himself after the leisurely fashion of Nature itself, and likewise never stopped working throughout his long day, not until his daily target of 500 pales or palings was achieved. If he managed it he went home with dancing feet; if – as very occasionally happened – he didn't he was plunged into despair.

Why twenty-five bundles of twenty each? I once asked as he began to fret he wasn't going to make it. Why not twenty-four? Or twenty? Why this arbitrary figure of twenty-five? He smiled, rather wearily, realizing how ridiculous it was to permit this self-imposed daily output to dominate not only his working day but his happiness, capable of turning his customary contentment into wretchedness, a sense of failure and hopelessness.

'Stupid, really, isn't it,' he poked fun at himself; 'but I can't help it. Funny thing is,' he stripped another piece of bark, 'it doesn't make all that difference if I do twenty-four or twenty-five, not financially. But I still can't help it. I've always been like it, since I started working in the woods with my old dad. He drummed it into me. Set yourself a target, and don't go home until you've reached it. Now I can't! And I don't really need the money any more, not to that extent.'

This idiosyncrasy apart, he loved working in the woods, and couldn't understand how anyone preferred being cooped up in a factory. 'I'll never retire,' he once laughingly told me, 'if only because I'd miss the trees, all this fresh air. And being on my own. I love my wife,' he added, 'but it's nice to get away. Sometimes.'

So much for the outlook of the craftsman pale-maker.

But what, you might well be wondering, has any of this to do with foxes? Well, in a word, everything. What follows is his eye-witness account of a distressing affair.

He was walking through the woods on his way home, having achieved his day's output, all 500 palings, when a hunting horn alerted him to the distant approach of some ten red coats and countless non-red going hell for leather. The howl of hounds, the thunder of hoofs, the rallying cry of the horn. Pandemonium.

Over the hedge in a field adjacent to the woods he

spotted a fox, trotting – yes, trotting! – totally unconcerned, seemingly contemptuous of these tiresome and
clueless disturbers of the peace.

The hunt was preoccupied with another fox a field and
a half ahead of its pursuers. A fox anything but lackadais-
ical. The hounds were gaining. Inexorably nearer. At this
rate the fox would soon be taken, possibly on the road
linking our village to the next and civilization beyond.

The huntsman with the horn almost blew himself inside
out.

The hounds closed in.

The pale-maker was galvanized.

Then a scream. A woman from one of two houses
backing on to the woods rushed out calling, pleading,
shrieking, sobbing.

Cats leaped everywhere, six, perhaps more, bolting into
the house. Still she called. Frantic. Hysterical.

The hounds hit the road, ignored the fox, and poured
into the woman's garden. One cat was too late.

The huntsman with the horn blew and blew. The
hounds ignored everything but their new prey. The
woman went berserk. The master of the hunt charged
into the garden, dismounted, looked stupefied.

The woman screamed at the master who screamed at
the hounds. The man with the horn stopped blowing.

The cat was in tatters.

Round the corner came a jogger, staying with relatives
for a few quiet days in the country. His mouth fell open.
He rushed into the garden, and rushed out again, appalled
by the sight. It transpired he was against fox hunting
anyway, as vehemently as the woman and her neighbour,
the latter now trying with only limited success to offer
comfort to the owner of the savaged cat.

Amidst this bedlam of threats and apologies, charges

and counter-charges, the gentle pale-maker's inclination was to say nothing, not to get involved. After all, the damage was done; the distraught woman, like her cat, was beyond human help, a reality brought into sharper focus by the master of the hounds' fumbling attempts to express regret. His distress was written all over the faces of the entire hunt.

But after their withdrawal, leaving a handful of onlookers to continue their diatribe against them and blood sports generally, the pale-maker, terribly sympathetic, of course, deploring the manner of the cat's end, nevertheless felt constrained to speak up for what he called 'this traditional part of country life'. Did the understandably outraged onlookers realize that of the thousands of foxes killed every year – estimated by some as 50,000, by other experts as high as 100,000 – only a quarter were dispatched by fox hunting?

Apparently they didn't; but such figures made absolutely no difference. What about the owner of the cat? they argued. Was all this talk about foxes needing to be controlled, and thereby paradoxically helped to survive, any consolation to her? The whole gruesome business should be outlawed. As was bear baiting. And cock fighting. And . . .

The pale-maker wasn't done yet. With more courage than he realized, he made the point that these things, including the unfortunate cat, needed to be looked at in perspective. What had just happened in a private garden was deplorable, in no way either tolerable or justifiable, but this was no reason surely to debar traditional hunting altogether!

'Fox hunting,' he concluded, 'doesn't appeal to me, any more than to you, but does this give us the right to dictate to other people, destroy something they claim to enjoy

117

and believe to be in the best interest of not least the fox?'

I gathered he remained in a minority of one. But such is the gentleness of the man I could well imagine that the onlookers, still vehement in their disagreement, couldn't take offence. The trouble was, he summed up his story to me, perhaps understating the case, feelings were running too high for a fair objective discussion!

'What about the jogger?' I inquired.

'Oh, *him*,' the remembrance brought a smile, 'he said something about going back to the peace and quiet of Canning Town. Nice chap. Claimed he was about to join the League Against Cruel Sports. Probably never seen a fox in his life.'

'Yes, what about the foxes, both of them?' I asked.

Now he really laughed. The one he'd seen first, trotting leisurely, had kept trotting, its scent obviously not picked up by the hounds. As for the other, it had been saved by the cat, forgotten long enough to get clean away. The hunt went home empty-handed after a hard day in the field. 'Can't say I'm sorry,' he concluded.

During the following weekend I had reason to visit the cottager's small-holding, and naturally mentioned the above episode. What puzzles me, I said, is where all these foxes hang out; and I admitted to my solitary sighting. His eyes filled with disbelief.

'Round here,' he declared, clearly in no mood to be contradicted, 'you can see 'em any time you want.'

I wasn't entirely persuaded.

'All you need is a bit of country know-how, nothing more,' he insisted. And he told me some cock-and-bull story about the old-fashioned way of seeing foxes.

'Tell you what,' he responded to my suspicion of leg

pulling, 'be at my cottage tomorrow night round about half-past-seven.'

We drove in his van for about a mile, certainly no more, to a part of the village circumference I knew well; been there often, not the smell of a fox. Within the next three hours we saw – I record in sober truth, still excited by the memory – five foxes, actually drawn to us by a simple technique passed on to countrymen for generations. It was uncanny. He spotted the foxes, all of them single sightings, and brought them to us until they were within twenty strides seemingly parading their magnificence for our inspection and admiration.

I returned to Hide 'n' Seek walking on air, baffled, exhilarated, feeling more of a countryman than ever before. Five foxes in one night! They coming to us rather than we going to them. Even my wife's scepticism was impressed. But what happened little more than a fortnight later did nothing to turn her into a true believer free of doubt.

We were tempted by a glorious sunset to take a quick walk before supper. Making our way to the woods, only a couple of fields from the cottage, we spotted a fox – incidentally my wife's very first sighting – also heading for the woods and scattering a flock of lapwings in the process.

'Go on, then', she encouraged, referring to the old countryman's technique.

The fox was already far ahead. I ran, at the same time trying to do what was required to attract its attention. The fox sped away and was soon out of sight.

'It couldn't have heard me,' I answered the question in my wife's eyes.

'You'll have to try properly,' she sought to soothe my embarrassment.

The woman was insufferable.

'What about later tonight?' I said.

We left Hide 'n' Seek soon after dark and drove to the spot where the cottager had parked his van. Following the identical route, we made our way past an old oast converted into a lovely home and currently occupied by a writer of children's stories, along a farm track and deep into the country.

Every so often I flashed the torch round the area, picking up innumerable pairs of eyes, all of them near enough to the ground to suggest rabbits.

We moved to a hedge, and swung the beam over the adjacent field. Nothing. We followed the hedge, and tried again.

'A fox!' I whispered.

It was on the far side, a distance, I should think, of some one hundred strides, staring straight into the light. In retrospect I'm not sure why I was so certain it was a fox, for we could see nothing but its eyes. But I knew!

Raising the back of my hand to my lips I started to suck, seeking to imitate, as the cottager had put it, a rabbit in distress, physically injured, open invitation to any predator to an easy kill and feast.

The fox moved towards us, just a few steps. Stopped. Crossed to the other side of the field. Stopped. Then came on apace, making no attempt to escape the beam. I sucked like mad.

What went wrong, at least from our standpoint, I shall never know, but suddenly the fox veered away and bolted, still some distance from us. Never mind. My wife was now convinced, utterly persuaded I hadn't been talking through my hat. We moved on, regularly sweeping the field with the beam, disappointed that for ten minutes or so we saw nothing but rabbits; scores and scores, compel-

120

ling me to appreciate why a farmer friend wouldn't complain if every single one of the species was removed from the face of the earth.

We reached a wooden fence, climbed it, followed a ditch, and swung the light over the hedge into the next field. A couple of sweeps, and my wife gasped. I swung back the beam, and there it was, another fox as clear as day peering into the light. Once more I sucked. Once more the fox responded, this time without apparent hesitation, until it stood within twenty or so strides of us, clearly perplexed by the whimpers of an invisible rabbit. And there it remained, wary, undecided, wanting to reach the easy kill but fearful of investigating nearer.

I sucked myself dry, so dry I couldn't suck any more. Still the fox lingered, for perhaps half-a-minute, before presumably detecting the ruse and disappearing. We followed it with the beam out of sight, then whooped like excited children. Whooped, I tell you. That moment remains one of the highlights, in some ways incomparable, of our time here; unrepeatable, the beginning of an altogether deeper, more intimate, involvement with the natural world. It was nothing, of course, not by the standards of a countryman like the old cottager, but for the pair of us it added a totally new meaning to living in the country.

10

Goats, sheep, and the stud farm quickie service

I only wish my enjoyment of foxes was reflected in our inescapable involvement with goats!

A quartet of them regularly roamed or plundered the fields round our cottage, a law unto themselves, pets more than stock belonging to a neighbouring farmer who doted on them. We've noticed this about goats. You either love them or hate them. And if the former you tend to go over the top.

Our neighbour kept them, I suspect, for reasons he himself didn't fully understand, but the official explanataion was his decided preference for their milk, a preference, I have to say, not shared by his wife, with equal emphasis. Fortunately they both loved goats' cheese, soft and hard, which they made about fortnightly by deep-freezing most of the daily pints – impossible with cows' milk – until the required eight gallons for another cheese-making session were available.

Meanwhile the goats continued to look longingly through or over the fencing surrounding my wife's treasured garden, their eyes on the love of their life, and hers – roses. The sight of them, wholly inaccessible, appeared to send the four marauders into a frenzy of desperation, the main reason why our fences were reinforced with barbed wire along the top, with a double push lock on the gate. Be warned. Never trust goats. Their delinquency is compulsive.

The mystery is, some people find even their roguishness irresistible. Certainly my wife felt little but affection for them, finally persuading the lot that her approach guaranteed ear kneading and other forms of indulgence.

One morning, early, the dawn chorus our only disturbance, the phone rang. The farmer wondered whether my wife's interest in his goats would extend to her milking them? Just the once. During the coming weekend. He was due to attend a meeting, and wanted his wife to go with him.

She went, my wife, for her first lesson in milking that night, surely the most eager volunteer in the history of goat-keeping. And she took to it, allowing, if you will, for the metaphorical mix-up, like the proverbial duck to water. Her first big surprise was the difference between milking a goat and a cow, making redundant all the advice I'd hurriedly passed on out of my conspicuous ineptitude at the cottager's small-holding. He'd showed me how to milk a cow. I'd tried with less than success, reducing the flow he'd produced to a trickle, but at least the technique had been firmly implanted; so naturally, confronted by my wife's enthusiasm I'd demonstrated how to transfer milk from animal to bucket with a cow firmly in mind. She'd practised on her imaginary goat, meaning that by the time she'd arrived for her first milking session her confusion was ripe for disaster.

At her first real lesson she was shown how to tighten her thumb and forefinger round the top of the teat, holding the milk in the teat, and how to use her remaining fingers to squeeze the teat firmly against the palm of her hand; never pulling, only squeezing.

I picked up these details as I watched her doing the milking for the first time on her own, Saturday morning and evening. When we arrived at the farmyard all four goats were waiting to welcome us, the bulging udders of the *two* milkers suggesting we'd put in an appearance not before time. As for the other two, much younger, their welcome was related to food, the main reason why all farm animals are happy to consort with humans.

The goats queued, impatient to get on with the routine. My wife allowed the senior goat, heading the queue anyway, into the milking area first, having reinforced its interest with concentrates (juicy nuts containing all the elements for a balanced diet). Hearing the generous ration hit the bottom of the bucket, the goat needed no persuasion to leap on to a platform some six inches high, stick its head in the bucket, and allow my wife to please herself! So far so good.

The apprentice milker then wiped the teats, carefully trapped the milk in one, and squeezed. Nothing. Not a trickle. Even a drop. She tried again, this time hindered as the goat, its mouth full of nuts, turned to look at what was going on or more correctly what wasn't going on.

Progress, it must be said, was slow, at times tortuous, but eventually the rhythmic beat of milk into the bucket indicated gathering success. My modest wife wouldn't wish me either to exaggerate or minimize the difficulty; I simply record that eventually, fingers aching, hands stiffening, back almost killing her, she came within reach of the final phase of milking called stripping, that part of the operation when a firm hand slightly lifts the udder to simulate a suckling kid struggling for the last drop, thereby encouraging the goat to let down any remaining milk. On paper it's elementary.

Never mind, the first goat done, in came the second, mad keen to appease its gluttony after being kept waiting longer than usual. It leaped on to the platform, goaded by the nuts hitting the bottom of the bucket, knocking both the bucket and the milker flying. I grabbed my wife, she grabbed the bucket, the goat grabbed the concentrates scattered among the straw.

Those juicy nuts were magic, in or out of the bucket, like a drug guaranteeing co-operation from a potentially obstreperous patient. And with this goat, the rogue of the quartet, the milker needed all the help she could get. Our own observations had long told us that this younger dam had been born to mischief.

Her instinctive reaction to a fence was to ignore it – either over, under or through, a veritable Houdini. Somehow we'd managed so far to keep her from our own garden, those few flowers nurtured by my wife in place of the hedge, but feared – I think accepted – that one day her ingenuity would find a way.

Yet it was impossible not to like her, or in my wife's case have even stronger feelings of affection. Her eyes could melt a heart of concrete – mine, for instance, sometimes – or defuse the most justifiable exasperation at her habitual bloody-mindedness. Being of the breed known as Anglo-Nubian, she had floppy ears, and legs that always struck me as being too long for her other proportions. What most endeared her to me was her capacity for silence. While the other goats occasionally exercised their vocal cords she never uttered a sound. At first I thought she must be dumb, even voiceless altogether, but this was before she came into season. You've never heard a goat calling? Be grateful.

However, fair's fair. Apart from the bucket incident, she behaved with unnerving helpfulness for her first milking by my wife; within half the time taken with the senior goat the whole operation was completed, leaving the triumphant milker with something like nine pints in total to reduce in temperature as quickly as possible, from eighty to less than fifty degrees Fahrenheit, to prevent the slightest possibility of infection.

She plunged the cooler into a sink of running icy water from the well in the garden, satisfied herself about temperature reduction, left everything spick-and-span, and strolled back to our cottage oozing goodwill. A human Cheshire cat!

And the pay-off? We both became addicted to goats' milk. And cheese. Talk about living it up in the country! As for the farmer and his wife, they were so impressed, by her efficiency no less than her enthusiasm, they henceforth recruited her services at the drop of a hat. Perfect arrangement all round.

There was another pay-off, still a memory of happiness tinged with sadness. We were, you see, given a sock lamb; not only the lamb but as much goats' milk as required for feeding, guarantee of a soon thriving orphan. In no time it was huge, ready to roam with the farmer's flock, part of the arrangement, but the lamb itself preferred human company, a danger for the unwary with farm stock. Seeing us anywhere on the farm, it would speed in our direction, utterly unconcerned about the farmer's sheepdog, another characteristic of a sock lamb. While the rest of the flock needed little persuading to fall into line, our lamb kept coming, apparently thinking of itself as more a four-legged human than anything else. Nice for us, but there was one major inescapable consequence the three of us would never have chosen.

Meanwhile, my wife and I were becoming increasingly aware of the meaning of lambing which on this farm started around 1 April and continued through to mid-June. The first time I saw a lamb actually delivered rather than naturally dropped happened one Sunday morning, shortly after first light. I was enticed out-of-doors so early by the weather, beginning of what proved to be a perfect summer's day. Our little bit of the world was waking; signs of life everywhere, not least in the countless nests in and around Hide 'n' Seek. Clearly we weren't the only ones to find the peace and quiet productive.

I strolled to the woods, and returned to the cottage about an hour later via the farmyard. The farmer and his wife were rather preoccupied. She was astride a teg – first lambing – lifting its bottom slightly off the ground while he pushed his hand further along the vagina seeking, I gathered later, to turn the lamb in the womb. The poor little blighter had come head first, impeding birth until the front legs were pulled forward. To an experienced shepherd the operation is normally straightforward, but on this occasion inexplicably the lamb wouldn't budge.

The farmer fitted a piece of cord round its head behind the ears, another piece round the feet, wound the ends dangling from the teg's backside round his hand, and pulled, careful to harmonize his herculean efforts with the contractions of the sheep. It seemed ages before the lamb fell to the straw. Dead.

I gazed at the tiny form, its head bloated and black, wholly disproportionate to its body. Grotesque. Beautiful. Pathetic. Why, I fumed, did nature play such dirty tricks?

The ewe, typically recovering in no time, sniffed the corpse, and inexplicably began to lick it clean. I looked again. Hard. Surely the eyes of that bloated head flickered. And the farmer noticed too, for quickly he removed mucus from the mouth and nostrils; and quietly watched the sheep, apparently indifferent to the size of the head, continue her licking. Within minutes the new-born was struggling to stand, and its awesome head was both beginning to shrink and change colour.

Later that same day my wife and I walked to the post-lambing pens to see the lamb with the big head. 'Which one is it?' she asked. And I couldn't distinguish it from the others.

The outcome of difficult births was not always so pleasing. A few days later I noticed the farmer carrying a dead lamb; still-born, he explained. He looked wretched, not – if you can follow his rather convoluted reasoning – because the lamb was dead, hardly a rare experience on even the best of sheep farms. No, he simply wondered – worried – to what extent he was responsible. Could he have done more, anticipated possible snags, kept the teg concerned under sufficient surveillance? For by the time he'd checked, the lamb was already on the straw in the lambing barn, totally ignored by the bereaved sheep from whose backside the afterbirth was still dangling.

The next time I saw the farmer he told me the postscript to this still-birth. He'd checked on recently born twins, already transferred to the post-lambing pens. Picking up the smaller one, sickly looking, more dead than alive, he quickly realized surrogate mothering was essential for even a slim chance of survival. Another sock lamb for his wife to nurse? Walking with it to the barn he remembered the still-born or rather the bereaved ewe.

Not wasting a moment he sharpened his knife and skinned the tiny corpse. With minor adjustments it fitted the sickly lamb like a glove. Then he brought in the ewe, and introduced the pair. She sniffed the lamb, turned away in disbelief, sniffed a bit more; and eventually started to lick her very own lamb, usual sign of total acceptance.

Incidentally, many vets think fitting the skin of a dead

lamb unhygienic, but as far as he was concerned, having tried newer ways, this traditional method couldn't be bettered. Certainly he'd never lost an orphaned lamb through infection from a dead lamb's skin, though admittedly the smell after a few days could sometimes be potent.

The adopted twin prospered and in no time, it seemed to us, was tearing about the pasture with the other lambs, all of them a picture of health, moving towards a day of reckoning we hadn't remoted anticipated. Of course, we knew with our heads that lambs went to market, but this was before our own sock lamb was ready to fetch the highest price. Leave it any longer, the farmer advised, and we'd get less, not more. *Now* was the right time to sell, along with his own next batch.

Within the next few days, never mind the day of departure itself, we realized we weren't the tough ex-townees we'd both imagined. We didn't see the lambs loaded and driven away – fortunately other duties called – but this didn't stop us feeling like a couple of traitors.

As consolation we decided, quite illogically, to buy a breeding teg, get ourselves personally involved in next season's lambing! By then our whole approach would be much more objective, dispassionate, hard-headed, a business proposition as much as anything else. So we bought Baa-Baa, bestowing such an undistinguished name on strictly logical grounds. She was black, The nursery rhyme said:

Baa Baa, black sheep . . .

I know! In retrospect we too wonder what in the world we were thinking about. At the time it was all simply part of the fun. For despite the departure of the sock lamb, we persisted in believing or acting on the assumption that farm animals, like living in the country, were essentially

129

fun, little short of a game; and in one sense for us they were – and so remain. But not in the stupid manner we thought about Baa-Baa at the time she joined us.

More to the point, naming a farm animal is half-way to getting too attached, too emotionally involved to make hard decisions with balanced judgement. The best farmers we know treat their stock with both kindness and dispassionate objectivity. If they name their animals at all – as some of them do – they take good care that this doesn't influence their business acumen.

That's the theory! Not so long ago, the old couple who met and fell in love at a barn dance, introduced me to one of their ewes soon to lamb for the thirteenth time. Yes, that's right – *thirteenth*!

Wasn't this rather unusual? I inquired, conscious of my understatement.

It was, agreed the farmer's wife. But she and her husband couldn't bear to part with this dear old friend; furthermore, she began to sound belligerent, why should they, while her lambs continued to be up to standard?

What happens, I asked, when she's past lambing?

We'll retire her to pasture, said the farmer. She's earned it.

And she didn't have a name, either!

But to return to Baa-Baa. The reason we'd chosen a black teg was the outcome of our neighbour farmer's idea. He thought this would help us to pick her out at a glance as she roamed the farm with his flock; reinforce our sense of ownership. And he was right. Each time we walked or drove through the farm, our eyes searched her out without difficulty; and this bond was further strengthened as we helped with dipping, hoof trimming, douching and dagging the entire flock, thereby handling her directly.

I won't say she recognized either of us with the same

130

alacrity, not in more than our imaginations, but we never doubted the special relationship between us, neither this nor all the joy we confidently anticipated through her.

Excitedly we watched the start of tupping – the release of the rams to the flock – and oozed satisfaction when within days Baa-Baa's rump was well and truly burnished with red raddling, sure sign of hope.

Meanwhile our involvement with the goats gathered momentum!

Floppy-ears the younger – the one I thought was dumb! – began to call. I've mentioned, perhaps you recall, a bulling cow. A calling goat is not so much louder as more piercing, guarantee of commanding attention. There were two other signs of her desperation. Her tail repeatedly twitched, increased by running a hand along her back, just to confirm; and the redness around her swelling vulva was accompanied by a mucus discharge. No doubt at all, she was in season.

Would my wife and I, the farmer inquired, like to take her to stud?

My wife guided her into the back of a van, I dropped the safety catch, and we were away, to an address on the far side of the village, a stud with a reputation for providing the satisfaction the fee warranted. We located the main gate, proceeded along the half-mile track, and found ourselves outside what looked like a row of stables.

Almost before we'd pulled up, out stepped a middle-aged woman bristling with efficiency. She glanced at the goat, assured us everything was ready, and led her away. Within minutes she was back, all smiles, asking for the fee.

My assumption was she expected payment before leaving the goat with the billy, but this merely underlined my ignorance. The goat had already been served! I must have looked what I felt – unconvinced. Artificial insemination was one thing, but this, a natural mating before I'd barely time to turn the van, was a bit much for even my gullibility.

If the billy's in the mood, the woman explained, he doesn't hang about; and this one, a new affection stole into her eyes, is always in the mood. Don't worry, he gave her, she nodded in the direction of Floppy-ears, an excellent service. Come back if it doesn't take. But I'm sure you'll find it has.

And while my wife returned the goat to the back of the van, and I counted out the stud fee, the billy's proud owner signed a certificate of pedigree.

The ways of nature are not always so straightforward! Not when an awful mystery, concern of the whole village for weeks, focused upon Bert Worth, beloved member of our normally quiet community. The firm gentleness of Bert himself was doubtless the legacy of his long experience of working with animals. Now retired, he and his wife occupied a tiny cottage on the border of the village, farmland on three sides, with a garden as colourful from spring to autumn as a patchwork quilt.

Every day if the weather was co-operative, and some-times when it wasn't, they could be seen pottering. More correctly, he pottered, she gardened. The reason for this distinction? Bert's eyes were wearing out. Even so, there was nothing haphazard about this pottering. Like his approach to life generally it was thoughtfully organized without a hint of either muddle or regimentation – a place for everything, everything in place.

Which explains why since the onset of his blindness his greatest fear was of becoming nothing but a potterer, more a liability than a help to his wife. And not only in the garden. Yet paradoxically, far from making him irritable or a moaner, his failing sight emphasized his graciousness and old-world courtesy.

Two other things were inseparable from remembrance of this old villager. First his Alsatian bitch, one of the keystones of his happy retirement. She certainly laid to rest my long prejudice against Alsatians; their reputation of being unpredictable with children and even occasionally biting if not amputating the hand that fed them simply didn't make sense in the presence of Bert's dog, as much the embodiment of strong gentleness as her master.

The second thing about him was his recent discovery of an unsuspected talent. Catching sight of him groping rather than seeing his way across the village green, you'd never think of him as an artist, yet the growing evidence spoke for itself, finally persuading modest Bert himself in perhaps the only way possible.

He submitted, aided and abetted by his wife, four of his latest pastoral watercolours to the regional society of artists and craftsmen for their annual outdoor exhibition, to take place at a nearby village as much renowned for its wealth as its self-conscious culture. Not only were all four immediately accepted for hanging, but separate buyers snapped them up on the very first morning.

Bert was still chuckling when he told me. £25 each. £100 for nothing! This man whose hands were calloused by a life-time of hard labour couldn't believe such a fortune could be made so easily.

But you see the problem for a budding artist of failing eyesight!

Bert never complained, at least not to my knowledge. I marvelled at his total freedom from self-pity. Listening to him you received the impression he was simply grateful his problems weren't more serious. He once laughingly told me he didn't need eyes any more than he needed words to communicate with his wife. 'I know what she's thinking,' he explained, 'and she reads me like a book. Makes for a quiet life after nearly sixty years together!'

Walking or driving through the village I often waved to them in their garden or stopped for a chat; but with the advent of colder weather they disappeared, and, to be honest, I forgot about them, a case I fear of out of sight, out of mind.

Other things too crowded in, not least the latest episode of the phantom killers. Three more ewes in lamb with their throats torn out. This dog-loving community can tolerate shit on the village green, but rogue dogs receive short shrift. I don't wonder the vast majority of farmers shoot the culprits on sight.

On this occasion a black mongrel was seen in the region of the attack, otherwise the killer or killers had again vanished without trace. Equally puzzling was the delay before the next attack. We knew it would come, for such a taste of blood generates its own murderous appetite, but as the days slipped away we began to hope the offenders had somehow already received their just deserts.

Evidence to the contrary a week or so later was no less gruesome. Two ewes killed, and another three badly mauled, their lambs almost certainly aborted. The farm this time was further from our village. I didn't know the farmer personally, but his young shepherd – the one who'd told me about foxes taking lambs – passed on the details, unnecessarily adding that if he discovered the guilty party he'd shoot without hesitation.

The next attack was barely under way when a tractor

driver, climbing from his cab to open a gate, heard the commotion a couple of fields away. As he ran shouting at the top of his voice he spotted two dogs which bolted, but not before he'd identified them without a shadow of doubt. One belonged to two ageing sisters living between our village and the next.

The other . . .

That afternoon a knock on the door of the cottage whose garden resembled the colouring of a patchwork quilt was answered by a man with myopia. He and his wife listened to the unbelievable. Yes, they had noticed blood round the dog's mouth, Bert admitted, but naturally it hadn't occurred to them . . . their only concern had been for the dog!

Hadn't they missed their dog, surely disappearing for an hour or more at a time? Not really, Bert's wife explained. What with the colder weather and her husband's failing sight, they'd taken to letting the dog out alone for exercise. Didn't seem right, the distraught seller of pastoral watercolours lamented, to keep her cooped up merely because they themselves couldn't get out. In any case, they knew she'd behave herself and come home when she was ready!

The farmer, a kindly man, wanted to be sympathetic, particularly in the face of the lovely couple's anguish. He knew how much Bert loved his dog, and didn't doubt his sincerity when promising with unconscious irony he wouldn't let the dog out of his sight. Alas, the farmer also knew such good intentions had no chance against a rogue dog.

Bert and his wife didn't argue overmuch. Their only consolation, if this isn't over-loading the word, was their own recognition and acceptance that in all the circumstances there was nothing else for it. But for an old artist and his wife who themselves wouldn't hurt a fly, and whose dog was the third member of a very happy trinity, the parting, he said, was worse than going blind.

11

Village pump politics and the windmill

In the pub shortly afterwards, talk was also of a once beautiful landmark plainly visible for miles around but now in ruins, glowering over the village in rebuke and protest. How come, some of the drinkers wanted to know, that a community proud of its history and heritage could allow its windmill built some 150 years ago slowly to fall apart? Were we so indifferent to the richness of the past, this monument peculiarly our own, wrapped up with the very identity of our village?

Better, others argued, the eyesore should be, if not removed, then left to disintegrate into oblivion, the sooner the better. Feelings were soon running high, often the way with village pump talk. We fully understand, mark you, people's concern about nuclear war and the value of the pound against the dollar, understand and wonder like everybody else; but weightier matters like village lighting, holes in the road by the church, the latest building application, and – as on this occasion – the windmill, take priority and bring out the best or worst in all of us.

Now I mustn't give the impression this was any sort of formal or controlled discussion. It took place as individuals played darts or skittles or propped up the bar or sampled the excellent food. But there was no doubting its earnestness, the passion and sometimes intolerance of the antagonists. They appeared to be split right down the middle, lifelong villagers and newcomers alike of all age groups evenly spread.

What about the cost? A retired civil servant tried to be businesslike.

Yes, what about the cost? Who pays? challenged the dissenters.

And when I heard the probable amount involved, I conceded they had a point; precisely a £30,000 point.

Even so, surely an enterprising community like ours could raise this amount?

Maybe. If we weren't already committed to fund the installation of a moderate swimming pool at the village school, and enlarge the village hall, both costly operations and needing the profit from every boot fair, jumble sale, whist drive, coffee morning, and barn dance in the neighbourhood.

Having myself often glanced at the crumbling edifice we called the windmill, I thought £30,000 a bit optimistic. More likely three or four times that amount. No way, retorted the would-be re-builders, explaining that most of the work could be done by volunteers in their spare time. We've plenty of craftsmen in the village who'd be prepared to lend a hand, they insisted.

There's craftsmen and craftsmen, the retired shepherd, typically courteous but, to my surprise, lining up with the opposition, confidently made the point. The young 'uns, he said, don't have the know-how of the old 'uns; never been taught. All those modern machines and things. Where could we find anyone to replace the great spur wheel, he displayed his knowledge, or the wallower? The old crafts are dead. In any case, this normally taciturn man summarized, what did our village want with a bloody windmill?

I couldn't believe it! This product of the village whose forebears possibly helped to build the windmill turning his back on its mooted restoration with derision. Not to

138

say aggression. Yet his very vehemence brought the discussion alive. Before, ideas and disagreements were exchanged with passion. Now, the issue became a matter of life and death, of community honour; and perhaps, as the sparks really began to fly, of only half-forgotten personal feuds and personality clashes.

At times I couldn't help but wonder where the windmill fitted into the discussion! Fortunately a cry from behind the bar, 'Time, gentlemen, please,' brought proceedings to an abrupt close.

The retired shepherd and I walked part of our way home together, and he was disarmingly candid about sentimentalists like me wanting, as he put it, to live in the past. You come here, he laughed, never more serious, looking for a way of life that died with the bullock plough, and thinking country life is a hayride creaking up the lane, children dancing round the maypole, roses round the door, that sort of thing. What you call the good old days. For some of us they were the opposite, bad old days, and not all that long ago, either.

His eyes burned with indignation. Who cares about the windmill? Let it fall down. It means nothing. I wouldn't, he concluded, lift a finger to help.

Little could he have realized that his uncharacteristically fiery words in the pub were already at work to frustrate, not support, his intentions. For listening, largely unnoticed, had been a young man, like the shepherd born and bred in the village. Leaving the pub, he made his way homeward via the windmill, one of his earliest memories, imprinted on his mind as inseparable from his happy upbringing. Gazing at the gaping structure, its giant sails gone completely, bits and pieces of them lying about, along with its fantail, the whole a sorry mess, he felt ashamed, a traitor to his past.

Something, he muttered to himself, must be done!

So. He called a public meeting in the village hall, a meeting widely publicized, meaning notices in the post office and our two remaining shops. Doubtless if the weather had been more co-operative the attenders would have exceeded the twenty or so who turned up, but any numerical sparsity was handsomely compensated for by the fervour of the windmill devotees. Presumably the dissenters expressed their opposition by staying away.

Yes, but what to *do* as distinct from merely talking? Indeed, could anything realistically be done? As much as we wanted to save the windmill we couldn't escape thoughts of the sum of money involved or the admittedly airy-fairy idea of finding sufficiently skilled craftsmen and women among us to do much of the work on a voluntary basis. At the end of many brave words we unanimously passed a resolution. To pass the buck. The local council was to be invited to come to our rescue!

We waited. And waited. Letters. Phone calls. And soon an alien thought began to penetrate. The mills of God were not alone in grinding exceeding slow. From their offices the officials concerned could hardly have been more sympathetic or supportive. Of course, they assured us, the windmill must be saved, if at all feasible. The next step was their visit to the site, not easy to arrange with all the cut-backs and pressure of other work. Nevertheless, rest assured . . .

Months later a date was finalized. Could a delegation of villagers be in attendance?

The two bureaucrats clambered over the ground floor, precariously climbed their way to the meal floor, what little there was of it left, and squinted upwards at the remains of the grain bins and upright shaft. They tapped the rotting wooden structure, mumbled reservations, asked about the hopper and stones and great spur wheel and quant, and queried whether something coming down from the floor above was the meal spout.

The inside was as much a wreck as the outside, and I found myself wondering what the men who had once worked the mill would make of its present dilapidation. To be honest, I also found it difficult to believe the mill had ever been a regional centre to which farmers for miles around had brought their corn for grinding. It stank of decay, a symbol of years of neglect. What had once echoed with the sound of turning stones and meal pouring into hoppers and bags for collection by wagons with their single horses or team of shires had become a mausoleum.

The men from the council promised a report as soon as possible. As professional negotiators they gave nothing away, apart from the modest opinion that a lot of work needed to be done if the windmill was to be saved. And the extent of this understatement was central to the report itself whose only virtue, from our standpoint, was its brevity.

The windmill must come down!

Did we realize, these gentle mandarins wanted to know, that the structure was highly dangerous, with a public right of way skirting the entire site inviting disaster? As much as they sympathized with our aim of saving the windmill, it represented a public hazard unacceptable to a responsible authority.

A demolition order was being prepared.

The reaction in the village was remarkable, not unlike a lover of peace and quiet finally pushed too far. The retired shepherd explained he still didn't care tuppence about the windmill, but couldn't stand these little empire builders telling the rest of us what we could and could not do. They should get off their arses and do something useful for a change, he fumed. And his views, more delicately expressed, were widely shared.

Demolish the windmill! Had the world gone mad? Didn't these vandals parading as public servants care about the irreplaceable treasures of rural history and heritage? Who the hell did they think they were anyway?

Meanwhile these maligned worthies, waving fistfuls of forms, prowled about the place promising imminent collapse reminiscent of the walls of Jericho. Furthermore, they apologized, they had the law on their side!

But did they?

A solicitor newly arrived in the village, as desperate about the windmill as befitted an ex-city dweller, dug into the records and discovered what the council officials had either overlooked or not understood. The windmill was a classified building. In other words, it couldn't be touched without permission of the Department of the Environment or some such body equally remote, guaranteeing at least a breathing space before the bulldozers moved in.

Since coming here I've often pondered what constitutes a village these days. It can't be simply a collection of homes in the country, for not all that far from here London-bound commuter residents of a growing housing estate surrounded by farmland proudly refer to their *village*, a designation they insist that bespeaks both their environment and life-style. They could be right, but any resemblance to a traditional village is restricted to the eye of the beholder.

A real village, it seems to me, needs living contact with the past. Many of the houses and cottages round our village green are, it's true, occupied by commuters, but not a few of them grew up here, and their forebears from generations back tramped these byways, ploughed these fields, worked these farms, tended these gardens; saturated the place with an indefinable spirit, sum total of the past, a past that often lies dormant – unsuspected, disregarded – until stirred or creaked into life by a proposed development at cross purposes with its essential identity. I can think of no other explanation to account for the campaign to save the windmill.

There were admittedly no marches of protest, no sitdowns or sit-ins, no signing of petitions. But things began to happen. Volunteers set about nullifying the council's main concern about danger to the public; scaffolding shot up, men of all ages crept about the structure like ants, pieces looking like broken wings came down or fell off, remains of the mighty sails were laboriously lowered.

Then a matriarch organized a knit-in, another stalwart sold chrysanthemums from his front garden; nothing spectacular or remotely suggesting the village was tottering into action. True, every hard-earned penny made the £30,000 target appear unreachable, but this paradoxically stiffened the resolve – some might say cussedness – in polite parlour no less than village pub.

And yet and yet . . .

We were stumped.

Plenty of us were used to run-of-the-mill DIY jobs like tinkering with engines or changing a tap washer, but restoring a complete windmill to all its first glory was somewhat outside our routine experience. Confronted by this towering rebuke to our years of indifference, we wondered what in the world to do next.

Mind you, we weren't lacking in theory. One of our number knew pretty well everything about windmills; his love affair with them went back for years, with an album of photographs taken by himself of the thirty or so in

Kent as evidence. But, alas, as any sex therapist will tell you, theory and performance are not always the same. The flesh was willing, but the practical know-how weak.

It was, I am authoritatively informed, at this precise point of our need that the influence of the village church began to assert itself. I have to confess I am a devoted non-attender myself. My sole aim is simply to record the developments centred upon the renascence of our windmill, an aim miles removed from claims of divine intervention and the like favoured by some villagers. The jigsaw of events can speak for itself.

The solicitor, a newcomer, as I've mentioned, to the village, continued to beaver away on the legal side.

The villager whose vision of a restored windmill was largely, certainly initially, responsible for the campaign gathering momentum, sustained his inflexible determination, refusing to take no for an answer from anybody, least of all distant bureaucrats.

A growing number of villagers kept the money rolling in and/or helped on the site, preparing the way for the actual rebuilding. Ironically this latter activity added to the headache, for the crumbling innards of the windmill shell underlined to what extent craftsmen of ancient skills were required. In the village they were conspicuous by their absence, and hardly likely, once located in regions beyond, to offer their services for a song.

It all looked hopeless.

Miles away, not a windmill in mind or sight, a civil engineer, a near life-time of executive responsibilities behind him, was considering his retirement. How to occupy his time? The problem was for him not only new but in one major respect frightening. He knew himself well enough to realize that without something practical to do, something involving the use of his hands, he'd be lost, on the scrap heap psychologically in no time. But could there be anything to do, if the wish he shared with his wife – a retirement cottage in the country – was fulfilled? Secretly he felt harassed and apprehensive.

Concurrently another engineer and his wife were coming home from an overseas appointment, bound for Kent, headquarters of his parent company, but unsure precisely where in the county they were going to live. All they cared about was to find a retreat to balance his hectic professional life.

Perhaps a picturesque village!

Still more miles away a diplomat soon to retire wondered with his wife about their future home. After years overseas their feelings were unashamedly nostalgic – 'Oh, to be in England . . .' – and the very word for them both evoked scenes of rolling downs, country lanes, spring lambs, cricket on the village green, primroses in the woods, meadows explored in childhood.

Three couples! They wrote to estate agents, followed up leads; and finally settled, two in the village itself, one on the outskirts, all three within easy sight of the windmill, barely aware of its existence before they arrived, little realizing, even suspecting for a moment, to what extent it was soon to regulate if not dominate their lives. To the engineers, notably the older, its restoration in every original detail became a personal crusade. As for the professional diplomat, self-confessedly hamfisted with hammer and saw, he set about demonstrating, for all John Buchan's quip about diplomacy always involving less than the truth, that the right approach by an experienced practitioner was capable of charming blood from a stone, gallons and gallons of the stuff in the form of hard cash.

To find the money was clearly not going to be the headache of our confident anticipations!

If all this additional immigrant enthusiasm wasn't universally popular in the village, I certainly didn't hear a word against it. On the contrary, not only was it both verbally supported and a shot in the arm for the already committed, but it led to the most surprising development of all. For as the steadily progressing work made more urgent our need for craftsmen skilled in the ancient arts, out, as it were, of the village woodwork emerged first one person, then another and another, each capable of miracles with museum-like tools. It was hard to believe! From under bushels of deceptive ordinariness lights began to flicker and then shine brightly, revealing the very talents we all thought largely dead and buried with craftsmen of long ago.

Of this élite group, old Tom Shoemaker, a name inseparable from our village for generations, was too frail to get to the windmill itself. So if Mohammed couldn't get to the mountain . . . Some of the work demanding rare skill was taken to a primitive workshop behind his cottage; and at his own speed, regulated by bronchial wheezing and arthritic joints, he renewed bits of the windmill's mechanism – teeth of the great spur wheel, the sack hoist, the wallower, the brake wheel, all the time concerned to rebuild and repair the old rather than completely replace.

Looking at Tom, listening to his always sparse words struggling for breath, you'd never suspect his hands were capable of such artistry. Yet time after time, confronted by something entirely new to his experience, a job reaching back to how things were done when the windmill was built all those years ago, he worked his magic. A master craftsman. And nobody would have known even Tom himself but for the windmill!

Tom wasn't the only revelation of hidden village resources. Somebody had the bright idea of inviting other local craftsmen and women to exhibit their work at a windmill open day; encourage them, and increase the smile on the face of our professional diplomat. For apart from the income he envisaged – 15% of everything sold by the exhibitors – he with the committee sought a wider appreciation of the way the windmill was being brought back to life; for gone completely was its glowering rebuke to our former indifference. The cap was already in place, indeed, most of the external structure was finished, resplendent in white paint, its first coat in any colour for donkey's years. The fantail and windshaft were scheduled to be slotted into position, and the mighty sails almost ready for hoisting, a moment keenly anticipated since the rescue's inception.

All the same, did we have enough craftsmen and women to put on a worthwhile exhibition? They weren't thick on the ground in our neck of the woods, at least not obviously. Which just goes to show their disproportionate modesty. For in the event, the weather co-operative, not only did they circle the windmill with examples of their skills, but many of them went one better and gave working demonstrations – the potter at his wheel, the lace-maker with her bobbins, the shepherd's wife with her spinning wheel, the hurdle-maker with his hazel strips, the basket-maker with his canes, the wood-carver with his mallet and chisels, not to mention a number of artists with their easels and palettes, and a calligraphist producing personal birthday and other greetings cards. Talent! Who would have thought it?

And people came from miles around, not, it's true, in their thousands, but certainly their hundreds for what proved to be something of a country fair. I'm not wanting to suggest that the £30,000 target was within sight, merely that the attested diplomat among us began to make encouraging noises.

It's hard to pin-point where things began to go haywire. You see, it's comparatively easy, take it from me, to re-build a windmill. To decide what to do with it once it's almost rebuilt is something else. Some of the villagers continued to claim the hand of God was at work at every stage. If so, He must have been rather short on actual windmilling experience.

It all started innocently enough with little more than leg-pulling between members of the restoration commit-tee. But almost before we knew what was happening, the village was split down the middle, both sides including lifelong residents and newcomers no less than old and young. No disagreement about our now pride-and-joy being made fully operational again, capable of grinding corn and bagging it, every single part of the entire edifice as solid and efficient as ever. Beyond this, however, passions ran high.

Just a little! Nothing personal, you understand. In fact, if you pressed me, I would say our village is no more pig-headed than any other, probably less so than most. Yet like all men and women of goodwill, we occasionally find it necessary to resist the inflexible among us who persist in their awkwardness.

Some said a full-time miller should be appointed: grind the corn, pack the flour, find the market, encourage fibre-diet fanatics to buy direct; foster a whole new industry for the village. We didn't want, they argued, a museum whose future belonged to the past. Let's finish what we set out to do. Restore the windmill to all its former glory – a *working* windmill!

Hang on a moment, urged the other side. Have we thought enough about the implications? Lorries using our inadequate roads to drop the corn; more lorries churning their way to collect the flour; more vehicles still with potential customers plus, of course, the many sightseers we hoped to attract. And what about the handful of nearby residents! How did they feel about this proposal to turn their tranquil setting into a main thoroughfare?

The question was little short of chicanery, for the villagers asking it, having done their homework, knew perfectly well that the people directly threatened were adamantly opposed. Not that this deterred the other side in the least. They all remained concerned that the good of the whole village was more important than the smug convenience of a few individuals. What about democracy, in any case? The vast majority of villagers beyond doubt wanted a fully restored *working* windmill, symbolic that we belonged to the future as well as the past!

'How do we know what the majority of villagers want?' The chairman, struggling to be neutral, felt constrained to fuel the argument. 'Perhaps,' he went on, 'we should have a referendum; settle the matter fairly. What do you think?'

'Have you thought of the cost? Just to find out what we all know.'

'But we don't all know.'

'Of course we do. Ask anybody in the village pubs, all three. They'd tell you.'

'Not everybody goes to the village pubs.'

'It's obvious. Who wants a windmill that doesn't work?'

'It will work. For exhibitions, school visits, special occasions . . .'

'You mean to tell me we've done all this work for nothing more than . . .'

'More to the point,' the chairman again quietly interjected, 'I'm not sure we could afford to run a working

149

windmill. Not commercially. There's too much involved.'

'Nonsense. We'd make money,' announced the man whose vision of a restored working windmill had initiated the whole enterprise. 'Make money,' he repeated. 'And the profit could pay for maintenance, an on-going problem otherwise.'

'Have you considered the cost of setting up this hare-brained scheme? A fortune. Even before we start. It's madness.'

'Why did we bother in the first place? What's the use of a half-finished job?'

'It won't be half-finished. We set out to restore the windmill, no mention of what is now being suggested. Another eighteen months or so at most and the job will be done – structure solid as a rock, sails in place, everything shipshape. How can you call that half-finished? I've been proud to be a member of this committee, but enough is enough. Once the windmill's restored, which is all we ever intended, I'm out. You can do what you like.'

'Let's sleep on it,' appealed the gentle chairman.

'That's the trouble with this committee,' challenged the inflexible visionary, 'far from sitting on the fence, some of us come down heavily on both sides.' He paused for his words to be taken to heart. 'In any case,' he sounded conciliatory, 'I have another proposal, one that could solve all our problems.'

The chairman looked at his watch. The diplomat gathered up his papers. Whatever the new proposal, this was perhaps not the opportune moment to share it. But the inflexible visionary ploughed on. And as he cast one verbal pearl after another, the emotional temperature rose higher and higher.

The owner of the land surrounding the windmill, he said, wanted to use some of it to build three or four houses. An application was already in to this end. If the windmill committee felt able to support it, the owner of the land had made it known he was prepared to give a sizeable portion of the immediate area to the windmill trust, thereby facilitating easier delivery of any corn for grinding, a necessity even if the windmill wasn't operated commercially.

'You mean we're being bribed!'

'Definitely not; and I resent the imputation. One good turn deserves another. The windmill benefits, that's the point – and no one can deny we need more housing in the village. Here's our chance to help on that front, and do ourselves a favour at the same time. The proposal is perfectly honourable.'

'It would ruin the approach to the windmill, absolutely ruin it. Don't you see! Since we've had a windmill, 150 years, its setting hasn't changed. Now you want a housing estate . . .'

'Really, Mr Chairman, this is nonsense. Three or four houses at most! They'd hardly be seen, make not a bit of difference to the approach or anything else. And what's the use of rebuilding the windmill if we don't show at least the same concern about maintaining the village? We need a balance – a working windmill to pay for its own upkeep, and more, not less, residents to support the life of the village; otherwise,' he hesitated meaningfully, 'what recently happened to another village shop will happen to the village itself, not to mention the immediate threat to our post office and the dwindling bus service, such as it is.'

The point was telling, but made no converts. The slight majority on his side before his appeal remained solid, but no more so than the slight minority in opposition, both sides reflecting their previous loyalties when discussing whether the windmill should be worked by a full-time miller or kept primarily as a showpiece for special occasions.

How it will all end is anybody's guess. Compromise is distinctly not in the air. Meanwhile the restoration of the windmill nears completion. The sails of unbelievable proportions have been hauled into place, and look absolutely magnificent. Persons still crawl about the scaffolding like ants, applying finishing touches, committed to nothing less than an authentic reproduction of the windmill as first witnessed.

Unfortunately none of this silences the polite acrimony within the committee room or clarifies the future. A nagging question won't go away. What's the use of organizing a grand re-opening ceremony if afterwards . . . ?

Talk about tilting at windmills!

12

The whippet man, and aliens in the dovecot

Controversy at the village pump does peculiar things to people, brings out at least the best in most of them. Men who normally wouldn't say boo to a goose are transformed. I wouldn't claim they started on this occasion to bang the table or even raise their voices; merely made it transparent that over their dead bodies would views contrary to their own prevail.

One of their number, taking us all by surprise, was the village whippet man, a term of communal affection if ever there was one. His instinct was to side with the rebels, but – seeing that the storm raging around the future of the windmill didn't lend itself to such an easy distinction – he brought his rugged independence of mind to bear in deciding to be undecided. Until the dust settled!

He was a great believer in letting the dust settle. Or, as he preferred to put it, 'giving it time to ferment', whatever the current 'it' happened to be. This attitude of waiting for things to sort themselves out, for him a positive philosophy of life, gave the impression he was easygoing, unconcerned about pretty well everything. Apart, that is, from his whippets. His ubiquitous pair, particularly after the death of his wife, were manifestly the centre of his world. Anything affecting *them* demanded decisive action. Otherwise, as I say, he supported the notion that problems usually resolved themselves, given sufficient time. Don't rush! he threatened.

I first met him without his whippets. We were on the only bus of the day, meaning one of our two buses a week, bound for the nearest town. Within minutes I knew he was a Cornishman, retired soldier, retired security guard, recipient of three pensions, nursing a sick wife, missing his family, the three girls married and miles away, homesick for Cornwall, but still in Kent in deference to the wishes of his wife, a local lass he married during his soldiering days.

He also told me, struggling to control his merriment at the remembrance, of a visitor to his little cottage the day before. His neighbour, an old-age pensioner living alone, newly arrived from the town, wanted advice. She'd just consulted the vet about her dog, main companion for some nine years, concerned that this admittedly indulged toy poodle had become lethargic, obviously out of sorts. The kindly man, characteristically unhurried, anxious to calm the fears of the owner as well as treat the dog, wrote a prescription and requested, just to be on the safe side, a specimen of the poodle's urine.

It was, in fact, only after the inseparables reached home that the true magnitude of the vet's request registered. Doubtless the poodle wanted to co-operate; but what to make of this new image of her mistress chasing her round the garden with a threatening object to hand! Frustration finally gave way to desperation, and, overcoming her embarrassment at introducing such a delicate subject, apologizing almost before she opened her mouth at causing so much trouble, the burdened newcomer confided her necessary task to the whippet man.

He looked at the dog. Its eyes were full of appeal. He looked at the dog's owner, her face flushed, her arms enfolding the love of her life. 'You'd better come in,' he said. And leaving the caller to talk with his wife, he took the poodle into the garden.

First he settled the dog, initially not able to bear her

mistress out of sight; then he gently ran the garden tap, almost encouraging the dog to drink; then he waited, a plastic receptacle at the ready. At the first sign of the correct posture he was over in a flash, relatively speaking. The dog beat him to it, or perhaps her flow was prematurely stemmed by the indignity of the container being pushed into place. Twenty minutes later the specimen was still proving elusive.

Eventually – the whippet man's alacrity and the poodle's aim mutually co-operative – a thimbleful of the desired elixir was obtained, to be borne triumphantly away by a woman who couldn't have looked more pleased, my informant insisted, had the specimen been gold.

Our shared enjoyment of this story somehow cemented our friendship, resulting inevitably in my introduction to the inner circle of perhaps the most fascinating breed of dog owners anywhere. But not fully until after his wife had died. Until then we never met by arrangement, rather stumbled into each other in our remaining village shop, or on the village green where he chatted to all and sundry, picking up news or gossip to take back to his wife.

Everybody liked him – for different reasons; the nobs because he represented the values they esteemed – fiery independence, proud military record of service to Queen and country, thoroughly reliable, hard working all his life, stable home, loving family ('backbone of the nation' a retired brigadier called him); the commoners because, well, he enjoyed a pint in the village pub, any one of the trio, played a fair game of darts, had no side, few complaints, was good for a laugh, and quick to lend a hand even to people he didn't really know.

When his wife finally lost her fight against many months of poor health we all felt involved. The problem was, of course, how to rally round without intruding, for at the centre of this free-and-easy Cornishman was a backbone of steel. The last thing he wanted was pity, less still patronage. Some of his neighbours tried to do more than he permitted; one or two, I suspect, were hurt by his brusqueness, never intended to hurt, but a bit off-putting if not understood. While he had breath in his body, he was fond of saying, he wanted nobody's charity.

The fact remained he was lonely, in a domestic world empty of people for the first time in his sixty-nine years. His daughters visited regularly, between them perhaps once a fortnight, but these happy occasions, though profoundly appreciated, were little compensation for the thirteen or so twenty-four-hour gaps between. What about his longing for Cornwall? The question misted his eyes. 'I've often thought about it,' he said, 'but the girls would have much too far to come . . . and anyway the people I knew back home are probably dead by now.'

There was, he said, only one thing for it. He would return to an early love in his life!

Have you, I wonder, ever met a genuine whippet man or woman, for the latter are at least equally involved? I mean the sort of person who not only eats, drinks and sleeps whippets, but sets about producing a champion? No! Then come with me for a stroll through our village.

The cul-de-sac on the left, opposite the post office, the end cottage – that's where our whippet man lives. Of course, he won't be in. Rarely is these days, not since he lost his wife. To find him we shall have to keep walking, past the church, down a sort of round-the-back footpath to the village green.

He's not there? Then we shall need to walk towards the next village, past an oast criminally being allowed to fall down, and on to a pub in no-man's-land. Not that we'll

156

find our quarry inside. Too early. He'll be either heading in that direction or coming back, by his side two whippets being prepared for a race this coming Sunday.

Their proud owner won't exactly be nipping along, due to an arthritic knee, but he's more than walking. Mark you, this is *exercising* the dogs, all the difference in the world, and a necessary preliminary to what is shortly to follow on the village green. Once there, on occasion before most of the village is awake, the real training starts.

I now know that most whippet owners don't bother with training their dogs even for races. They treat them as pets, no more, take them to an open space for a daily romp, and let the racing take care of itself. If they win, they win; if they lose, who cares? No pressure, no aggro; it's all good fun and part of a marvellous family outing. Incidentally, no betting, no paid officials. The sport is in the hands of the owners themselves whose self-admitted fanaticism appears to include the belief that this breed of dog explains the purpose of creation. The only difference between them and our whippet man is that he thinks his pair more deserving of praise.

Anyhow, we've now arrived at the open space where occasionally I've assisted with the workout. How? I hold the dogs while the whippet man backs away clearly within their vision. When he says the word, I release them, and they shoot to his waiting arms. You wouldn't believe such tiny dogs could achieve such speeds.

These training sessions sound primitive, and doubtless, by professional standards in, say, the greyhound world, they are, but they work effectively enough for our whippet man who in any case wants nothing remotely to do with greyhounds. (I once innocently referred to his pair as miniature greyhounds; only the once!)

157

Then – frequently instead of the bursts of sprinting – we make for the river. Which brings me to their second remarkable characteristic, in some ways more impressive than their speed. I always thought Jack Russells, another tiny dog, were unique in terms of ferocity to size. To watch them deal, for instance, with a rat or a fox is a revelation, at least to ex-townees like me. But hardly less surprising is to witness a whippet dispatching a rabbit or a stoat. Awesome. And there was absolutely nothing we could do to stop this natural savagery.

Our whippet man, a real softy with all animals both domestic and wild, hated his dogs to pounce, and wretchedness would be written all over him as, like lightning, they shook the life out of their latest quarry. 'I wish they wouldn't do it,' he used to say, 'but it's bred in 'em, you see. You can't blame the dogs.' And with this as slender consolation, he left the victims to nature's great re-cycling process. 'My wife,' he once told me, 'couldn't understand why I didn't bring the rabbits home for the pot; she made a lovely pie in our early days when you could buy a wild rabbit for a few coppers. But the dogs killing 'em, I don't know, it's not the same somehow,' he'd smile, embarrassed.

That's as maybe. But beyond doubt his couple of whippets, ruthless killers by breeding or not, helped him through his grieving and initial unbearable loneliness. For without them – left with nothing he *had* to do – he would, as he himself confessed, have been tempted to throw in the towel, hide on the inside of his own front door, and fade away from self-pity.

As it was, the dogs, whatever his inclinations, needed to be exercised! This prised him from the cottage, to meet people willy-nilly, the very thing he didn't want but in retrospect recognized as being his salvation. And soon, his decision firmly made to race the dogs at club championships on the other side of the county, he found himself possessed by new meaning and, once more, joyful anticipation.

The day of the races began bright with promise in more ways than one. The sun invited optimism, the car started after a few teasing moments, and we set off like a pair of conspirators confident with unacknowledged doubts of total success. An hour and a half later we pulled off a meandering lane into a field surrounded by farmland, the field packed with cars and vans displaying a common insignia:

CAUTION
This vehicle is transporting
racing whippets!

Not that we needed such confirmation of our arrival at the right venue. Whippets were everywhere, far more numerous than their owners whose commitment to the breed manifestly can't be all that unlike the problem facing the alcoholic – one taste and you're done for. Pairs, trios, quartets and quintets paraded their handlers to the weighing shed where each dog, surrendering without the least protest, was suspended in a harness from the scales to confirm its poundage remained within its classification of race. The only other category was comprised of veterans, dogs of six years plus (rarely more than nine) which were handicapped by their age and weight.

The whippet man's dogs were in the classes not exceeding eighteen pounds and twenty-one pounds respectively. We knew the heavier dog, often outpaced in workouts by the younger dog, didn't realistically have a chance; but surely the eighteen-pounder did. An outside chance. If she performed at her best.

Not that it mattered one way or the other! We were agreed the main thing was the sport itself, fun for everybody, winners and losers alike. But waiting for the racing to begin, the whippet man, typically unperturbed, admitted he shared my desperation for victory.

The deadline for the weigh-in was midday. We found a quiet spot to eat our sandwiches and finish two flasks of coffee, content to observe the camaraderie of whippet owners and their families greeting old friends, creating a carnival atmosphere that quickened our own excitement. A puppy with its left front leg in a splint hopped past, its eyes rarely away from its doting owner, a woman no longer young, who smiled and asked whether we'd like a copy of the *Whippet Times*? Pocketing my twenty pence change from a pound, flipping over the pages, I admitted I didn't myself own a whippet.

She couldn't have appeared more shocked had I confessed to being a carrier of the plague. And then her horror turned to pity and sympathy and commiseration, underlined as she related the story of her own love affair covering many years, unaffected by whether her dogs won or lost, even raced at all.

'They're such lovely pets,' she said, 'loyal, affectionate, no bother. You really must get one,' she instructed.

The tannoy announced the first race, for dogs up to sixteen pounds.

'What about training,' I asked, 'don't you find this a tie?'

'Training! I never trouble,' she said; 'take them for a walk every day, that's about all. They don't need special training, not unless you want to win the open,' she laughed, 'and I certainly don't. Most of these owners,'

160

she looked over the milling crowd, 'give their dogs a daily walk, like any other breed. Whippets love racing, run their hearts out if you give 'em a chance. They don't,' she repeated, 'need special training.'

Once more I glanced at the whippet man's programme. His lighter dog was in the third of one hundred and forty races, all within four or so hours, involving, allowing for heat winners running again, some three hundred dogs, I reckoned.

The first five dogs were pushed into the starting trap, a signal was given, and the simulated rabbit was on its way, round a two-hundred-yard course shaped like a flattened half circle, lovingly staked out that morning by voluntary helpers on the club rota.

The winning dog was streets ahead of the others in a time of 13.1 seconds. Once over the line it was allowed to pounce on the 'rabbit' which naturally kept all five runners ecstatically occupied while their owners hurried from the starting trap to reclaim them. I immediately found myself more interested in the owners than the dogs. Their faces! Radiant. Disappointed. Embarrassed. Who said winning or losing made no difference?

Already the whippet man was at the starting trap, waiting his turn as the dogs of the second race were pushed into place. My heart was thumping. I felt apprehensive. Having often seem him giving his dogs a run, I knew they were fast, but having watched the first race, five dogs flat out in controlled competition, two thoughts were uppermost: no longer did it seem unbelievable that, pound for pound, whippets were faster than greyhounds, as I'd often been told; and – more ominous and worrying – the faster of the whippet man's pair would have to be on her very top form to stand even an outside chance. As for the other dog, I could only hope – squirming for my lack of faith – she wouldn't get lost finding her way round the course.

The dogs for the third race were now in the trap. The 'rabbit' was on its way. The excitement!

A memory flashed in my mind. As a lad of fifteen I'd watched a grey stallion in the parade ring at a point-to-point meeting, certain it was going to win. My older brother having placed our two bob *each way*, a concession on my part to his excessive caution, we watched from the back of a lorry parked near the main stand, and offering an excellent view of the entire course.

Immediately the race started I was on the horse's back, charging to the first fence, and the next and the next, always up with the leaders, not beaten until the final jump; the cheapest two bobs' worth of blissful nerve-racking uncertainty I'd ever known. And here I was experiencing the same emotional intoxication as I waited for five howling canine rockets to be launched.

It was all over in too few seconds for our ambling beauty. To be fair, she finished the course, and doubtless would have joined in the 'rabbit' pouncing merriment over the line, but by the time she arrived the artificial quarry was on its way back for the next race.

I can't exactly claim we didn't care, merely felt the sky had fallen in. To be honest, we were more concerned about our other dog, due to race within minutes, fearful she might lose sight of the other four competitors, never mind the rabbit. But I mustn't exaggerate. It didn't really matter who won or lost.

I was left in charge of our speedier loser as the whippet man queued behind the trap, moving nearer each time five more dogs were on their way. The dog by his side looked perky enough, indistinguishable from the others, yet the alien thought wouldn't go away – if she couldn't beat our loser, how in the world could she cope with the quartet waiting with her to be pushed into the starting trap?

Ironically, it was at this demoralizing moment that I found myself laughing out loud, provoked by the memory of Alan Bennett delivering his satirical sermon in the revue 'Beyond the Fringe':

> For when the One Great Scorer comes
> To write against your name,
> He marks – not that you won or lost –
> But how you played the game.

Hearing him the first time, I nearly did myself a mischief; now the memory, not recalled for years, enlivened proceedings as I awaited the ignominy of the race about to start.

The dogs in the trap howled their impatience to be off. The 'rabbit' was on its way, now level with the trap, now tantalizing the dogs as it sped ahead. They were still bunched at the first bend. And the second. Down the straight two were neck and neck, and collided heavily as they pounced on the 'rabbit', joined almost immediately by the others, a whirling mass of whippet ferocity.

Owners rushed and grabbed. Only one dog remained to be claimed. Hearing the whippet man's voice, she bolted in his direction, missed him, jumped a rope marking the course, and darted in circles, unable to locate him. Then he scooped her up in his arms, his face a study – of what it feels like to own a winning whippet.

Mind you, we always knew she was a winner! At least this was the gist of our enthusiasm as we waited for the semi-final. A born winner! If only we'd gone home there and then, nursing our illusion, unbothered that the fastest dogs from the other heats were poised to expose our pretensions. Would this, I subsequently conjectured, have made our disappointment any more bearable?

Less uncertain was the reaction to the semi-final result of the whippet man himself. Which explains why, if you happen to pass through our village these days, you might come across not two but four whippets by his side, each of the additions reputed to be unbeatable. Whether this sober judgement also applies to their racing speed is yet to be tested, but beyond peradventure they've already helped their proud owner to win his own far more difficult test of grief and loneliness.

For a reason wholly unrelated to the whippets, I shall always remember those first races. Our homeward journey! We talked not dogs but doves. And starlings. What to do about them, if anything? The dovecot had four sections, each one big enough for a couple of doves, ideal for breeding. The pairs knew their own place, and appeared not to want to intrude on the others. From this standpoint, at least, peace and harmony ruled.

Or did – until a couple of starlings decided to move in!

I wasn't impressed. Starlings, despite their undeniably beautiful plumage, despite their alternative names of sheep stare, shepster and sheppie, originating in their tendency to patronize the backs of sheep to pick off nourishing ticks, an idyllic image, seemed committed to safeguarding their widespread unpopularity. My own tolerance of these bullyboys of the bird table was never more than reluctant. Not only did they keep smaller birds at bay, but further postponed general feeding by lingering to preen their arrogance as much as their glossy feathers. Their capacity too for corporate defecation was hardly endearing, not when the car was newly cleaned, as I had every reason to know. So their activities at the dovecot justified my growing antagonism!

Nevertheless, undeterred least of all, it seemed, by the doves, they continued their feverish nest building.

The doves fluttered their protest to little effect; clearly resentful, at times provoked mildly to defend their own. I visualized all manner of dire consequences if once the squatters gained a nesthold, but hesitated to interfere, exasperated by the acquiescence of the doves, hopeful the starlings would realize there simply wasn't room in one section for two pairs. They didn't, unless assuming the doves would be the first to yield. Eventually – feeling my first responsibility was to the sitting tenants – I heaved out the nearly finished nest.

The starlings immediately started again, barely a moment's hesitation. 'It's no use,' a neighbour told me, 'removing the nest unless you burn it or put it in the dustbin; otherwise,' he laughed, 'the little blighters will use the same materials time after time.' I burned it. They found other materials. I removed a second nest. They built another.

By now a state of war existed, neither side prepared to budge. It was as though the starlings, once having committed themselves to build in a particular place, were incapable of changing the location. Their tenacity was both infuriating and admirable. Even the doves bestirred themselves. Whereas in the early stages they appeared largely indifferent or perhaps not sure how to cope with such audacity, the pair directly concerned, notably the cock, took defensive action. The hen was otherwise preoccupied, for even *before* the starlings started their building, she was sitting in her own nest on a couple of eggs. Which was another puzzle. Why this section of the dovecot when the other three were empty for a major portion of each day?

None of it made sense.

The seesaw contest continued for some five days until the intruders, finally persuaded they weren't welcome, transferred their industry to another section!

The doves now involved were less accommodating from the word go. Taking turns, they blocked the entrance, big enough for only one dove at a time, by sitting across it, no possibility of admission. The starlings, undone for about five minutes, no more, continued their building. One, its beak stuffed with nest materials, waited on a nearby silver birch; the other buzzed the sentinel, not a moment's peace, keeping it sufficiently harassed for the other to nip in – once, I observed, actually between the guardian's legs! – guaranteeing the building continued apace.

I was outraged. As much as I admired this ingenious penetration, I didn't want a dovecot of starlings. But what to do? All I could think of was to keep heaving out the nest materials, and hope the doves would improve their defences. They appeared to try, cooing defiance, stabbing with their beaks at the starlings' approach, intensifying their futile fluttering, but all to little purpose; the squatters strengthened their nesthold, stopping only at night, when the two doves, together claiming their own for roosting, made further access impossible by filling all the space available. The next morning, however, by the time I glanced through the bedroom window, the starlings were back, waiting with stuffed beaks for the doves to leave for feeding.

Where would it all end? I wondered. Two whole weeks after their initial sortie, the starlings were still at it, not a sign of discouragement on their side. On the morning of

166

the whippet races I ripped out their latest nest, knowing full well they'd start building again immediately my back was turned.

The whippet man listened to my tale of woe, his eyes smiling as I made the point that the dovecot was intended for our pleasure, not the invaders' convenience.

'Starlings, you say! In your dovecot!' His voice was, I detected, amused, slightly mocking though not offensive. 'Tell me,' he said, 'how would you feel if the culprits were blue tits? Not that they'd try to build in a dovecot; that's not the point. How would you feel if they did?'

'I'm be charmed,' I didn't hesitate. 'Charmed.'

'Vicious little buggers they are,' he said, 'as bad as starlings for their size.'

I wasn't sure he was serious.

'Ever seen them kill? A bee, for instance?' he asked.

'A blue tit!' My disbelief protested.

'A proper little butcher bird,' he said; and proceeded to give a lurid blow by blow account of how this adorable bird purposefully hung about at the entrance to a hive to pick off a victim and beat the living daylights out of it against twig or branch. And why not? he concluded. Blue tits need nourishment; nothing tastier than a juicy bee. It's not nature's way to mollycoddle.

Having waited for this hard truth to dissolve in my mind, he reverted to his basic philosophy. 'Don't interfere,' he said, 'let the doves and starlings sort it out for themselves. You'll see!'

'How would you like blue tit to nest in the dovecot?' I asked my wife on reaching home.

'That would be nice.' she said.

'Do you realize . . . ?' I began.

So we accepted the whippet man's advice, and waited.

167

And watched, from an entirely new perspective; captivated by the starlings' tenacity, puzzled by the bigger pair's apparent inability to safeguard their own. How was it resolved?

The starlings persisted, persisted as though, as I say, having commenced building in this particular place, they were incapable of not finishing, driven on by an internal gyroscope over which they appeared to have no control. As for the affronted doves themselves, they decided, fortunately, no doubt, to make a virtue of necessity as the starlings steadily made headway. The hen laid a couple of eggs in the starlings' nest! Bingo. The flummoxed starlings finally gave up, and were last seen with stuffed beaks beyond the ancient barn.

All we had to do now was, in the fullness of time, safeguard these latest dovecot fledglings from Leo and his kind. *We* safeguard the fledglings? Another case, I wondered, of our interfering with Nature?

13

Insects, and the badger that rose from the dead

On the other hand, what about Nature interfering with us, interfering first to irritate then to infuriate? Virtually everywhere, but particularly in the country, a multiplicity of insects invites interest or insanity; offers the choice of greater understanding or being driven mad – both, until you apply yourself to more than hunting them down. I was increasingly coming across all manner of creepy crawlies in the garden, in the cottage, on and around the pond, by the river – and being irritated not only by their bite or buzz but my appalling ignorance of their identities and less pestilent ways. For of all the many things I didn't know about natural history, insects easily headed the queue.

And the same applied, I was surprised to discover, to all the old countrymen and women whose wisdom, apart from this one area, was a constant source of enlightenment and pleasure. The world of insects – forget the blowfly and cockroach and colorado beetle and woodworm, destructive species usually related to routine work – was to them, too, largely a closed book.

'Why not,' suggested my wife, herself more than contented to recognize earwigs, mosquitoes, ladybirds, silverfish and the like, 'seek the help of an expert?' She was referring to a professional entomologist who, a short ride away, ran occasional weekend courses. So taking, as it were, the wasp by the horntail, I applied.

The very first morning, Saturday, he handed me a scoop and a pooter, the first to gather up the insects, the second to suck them into a bottle for subsequent examination under a microscope. Easy, he insisted; just scoop through nettles, long grass, any vegetation you come across. You'll be amazed how many you capture. And having deftly demonstrated his meaning of *scoop*, he abandoned me to instruct another innocent, confident I couldn't go wrong!

Feverishly I scooped, just as he'd showed me, never for a moment doubting I was about to be exposed as an uncompromising guarantor of insect liberty. What surprised me was the vehemence of my hunting. Until now I thought myself as compassionate, incapable of inflicting unnecessary pain on any creature; but the feared humiliation of catching nothing fired me to plunder the undergrowth and wave my scoop like a human windmill.

The extent of my success was astronomical. I knew, from my reading of Michael Chinery's marvellous insect book, there were 750,000 different species of which 20,000 plus could be found in Britain, but never at my most optimistic did I expect to catch more than half the first time I tried. Yet here they were, apparently the lot, jockeying for space in my bulging scoop. Amazing.

This was no time to hang about. I grabbed the pooter; and began to realize there was more to transferring insects from bulging scoop to specimen bottle than meets the eye. By the time the instructor returned, my bottle – apart from three and a half specimens – was as empty as my now deserted scoop.

'Having trouble?' He minimized my difficulties; and proceeded to over-simplify the method of transference. 'In trying to escape,' he said, 'insects always fly upwards, never down. Always *up*,' he emphasized. 'So if you put the scoop over your head like this,' he disappeared up to his shoulders, 'you'll be able to pooter, pick off what you want at your leisure, no trouble at all. Otherwise,' he shrugged, 'most of what you catch will get away. Try it!' he encouraged.

Once more I swept the scoop through nettles and their surrounds, gratified at the ease with which it filled with creatures great and small, some crawling, most flying. A smart twist of the wrist sealed the scoop. All I had to do now, in one intrepid movement, was pull it over my head.

The crescendo of buzzing suggested the captives' anger was looking for human flesh on which to vent itself. I peeped into the scoop. A few escaped. Not enough. Thousands, it seemed to me, remained. I glanced across at another hunter, disappearing into her net, pooter at the ready. Indeed, she positively plunged in, apparently indifferent to the inescapable invasion of her hair, ears and other orifices of body and garments.

Taking myself metaphorically by the scruff of the neck, I brought the full weight of my cowardice to bear. Wouldn't it be more sporting, less cruel, to offer a more than even chance of escape? Take only half-a-dozen of insects disposed to patronize the specimen bottle? In any case, what did I want with legions of legs crawling all over me? Persuaded by such humane logic, I opened the scoop, stood back as a black cloud rose like a mushroom, and pootered the stragglers that remained, a glorious galaxy of the commonplace. Sheepishly I made my way back to the lab.

We were each given a low-power stereomicroscope, and instructed how to identify our specimens by following the *key*, a simple step-by-step choice of narrowing alternatives to track down first the order, then family and genus of the specimens. Altogether there were forty-seven sets of alternatives.

1. Insects winged?
   Insects wingless or with vestigial wings?

   If winged, proceed to question 2.
   If wingless or with vestigial wings, question 28.

2. One pair of wings? – to question 3.
   Two pairs of wings? – to question 7.

3. Body grasshopper-like, with enlarged hind legs and
   pronotum extending back over abdomen! – see p.78
   Insect not like this? – to question 4.

Get the idea! It might seem complicated, but even a
born non-entomologist like me found it only bewildering.

Tenderly I picked up the first of my specimens, and
peered down the microscope, my very first experience of
such magic. The transformation of the small black non-
descript into a monster of intricate detail was barely
believable. I stared, galvanized, incredulous the creature
I'd examined with the naked eye was the same one. All
this fantastic ingenuity into the making of one tiny insect
of 750,000 species.

Now to identify it!

My insect had wings; two pairs, front ones horny except
for membranous tip . . .

The man asked me how I was getting on. 'It's a bug,' I
replied, adding for good measure, 'of the order
Hemiptera.'

'Look again,' he said.

I followed the key from the beginning, and reached the
same conclusion. 'It *is* a bug,' I confirmed.

'A bug,' he corrected, 'has only one pair of antennae;
your specimen has two pairs.'

I peered down the microscope, checking and re-check-
ing. 'There's only one pair of antennae here,' I said.

He came round to my side of the desk and peered down the microscope. 'I'm afraid one pair,' he sounded sympathetic, 'is missing; must have been knocked off in transit. Happens occasionally . . .'

'So what about the key?' I said.

'Get another specimen,' he counselled, 'and this time be sure it's all there.'

'Yes, but how do I know . . . ?'

The green insect next in my queue certainly looked all there right enough. And under the microscope it struck me as perfection – breathtakingly beautiful, a work of engineering genius. I looked and looked, most of all at the transparent mottled wings whose veins, invisible to the naked eye, wove a sort of crazy paving of flawless symmetry.

Eventually, feeling rebuked at my meddling, I turned to the key, and identified the beauty as a green lacewing of the order *Chrysopidae*, sometimes called golden-eyes because of a brilliant metallic appearance. But what's in a name? I wasn't sure any more that the sheer numbers of green lacewings justified the sacrifice of a single one to satisfy my curiosity.

Less problematic was my immediate addiction to the microscope, and not only because of the insects. A fellow budding entomologist on the course, sufficiently experienced as an amateur naturalist with professional standards to be trusted with our instructor's own superior microscope, solemnly informed me I must buy one for myself. No argument. His own, he explained, had transformed not only his retirement but his life. And maybe his marriage. For his wife, having peeped down his, had wanted one for herself, his never being available to her, and now they didn't have enough long winter evenings to explore this new dimension of entertainment. 'You won't have to worry what's on TV,' he laughed, 'if you get one.'

He and I were standing, only the two of us, at the edge of a wood, having just examined the various traps we'd set up earlier in the day to ensure a steady supply of specimens. Business was satisfactory from our standpoint, but he was more concerned to enthuse about the microscope than the number of corpses awaiting our attention. His first interest was, he explained, archaeology and pollen deposits from ancient sites or bogs to indicate the flora and fauna of former times. 'Analyse the residual pollen,' he said, 'and you have a picture of the landscape.'

He paused, smiling at my obvious astonishment at this for me totally new idea. 'As I grow older,' he continued, 'I find myself, like most people of my years, I suppose, asking more and more questions. How and why?' He bent with indecent haste for a man in his seventies, and plucked a single leaf of a stinging nettle. 'Do you know how this stings?' he asked. With understandable care he folded it and held it up to the light to expose a series of minuscule spikes along the centre vein at the back. 'You see,' he pointed to them, 'these penetrate the skin and exude their noxious defence. Never knew *that* for years.' He cast the leaf aside, and picked a single head from a cluster of lesser celandine. 'Come and have a look at this,' he invited, leading the way back to the lab.

I stared down the superior microscope belonging to the instructor. 'See the stamens?' the old man whispered, his voice alive with excitement. 'How many?' I counted them without difficulty. 'Now look at the pollen. How many particles? Would you believe it? Better than the telly, isn't it!' he declared. 'Take it from me, you'll never be lost for something worthwhile to do if you get yourself a microscope.'

I knew he was absolutely right.

174

Until he told me the price.
Meanwhile the telly isn't all that bad.

My interest in insects was firmly quickened by a roadside casualty I came across on the outskirts of the village. Heavy tyre marks on the grass verge indicated the vehicle – a lorry of some sort by the look of things – had braked desperately and swerved. To no avail. I was appalled. And astonished. For until that moment it had never crossed my mind we might have a badger sett in our immediate neighbourhood. Yet here was a dead badger, presumably killed crossing the narrow road, and lifted by someone to the hedgerow.

No one had ever seriously mentioned badgers to me. There had been reports of a sett half-way between our village and the next, but the source of my information, a young shepherd with more interest in sheepdogs and Jack Russells than badgers, had agreed to join me in a search for it without success. Signs of a sett ever having been there had proved inconclusive – a couple of sizeable holes, reputedly entrances, but these could have belonged to an old earth. More to the point, badgers were clearly not in residence now.

I gazed at the dead badger. Inwardly I wept. OK – so I'm an ex-townee sentimentalist; but the sow looked to be in lactation, with what consequences to her cubs I could only imagine. This apart, the mangled remains of such a lovely creature were somehow indecent, an outrage. I didn't doubt the accident was probably the badger's own fault, unavoidable by even a careful driver, and obviously lamented – hence the trouble to stop and lift the body off the road – but none of this remotely relieved my feelings.

Despite the accident, the corpse's coat indicated the animal's fastidious concern for cleanliness, accentuated by the streaks of white round the face, and the glossiness generally. Blood-stains suggested the head had been the direct point of impact. I suppose I stood there for ten minutes or so, my mind racing, feeling I ought to do something, knowing there was nothing I could do.

The badger was dead, this much was self-evident, yet I still found the scene difficult to comprehend – the total surprise of coming across a badger at all relatively near Hide 'n' Seek. It didn't seem feasible, not when badgers had never been suspected of being in the area.

Each time I passed the spot – and I found myself drawn, going out of my way to do so – I paused for another look, a token of respect, still incredulous the corpse was a badger. More incredulous still, I wondered after about four days whether this badger was a corpse at all! For as I gazed, it moved. The eyes. The mouth. Moved, I tell you, as though the poor creature was struggling to live, emerging from unconsciousness. And closer inspection confirmed the presence of life.

I looked again, no longer unsure.

On arriving home I turned to the key for identifying insects, and there it was, the information I needed. For the signs of life in the dead badger had resulted from the egg-laying capacities of a species of *Lucilia*, a fly commonly known as a greenbottle, sometimes called a blowfly or bluebottle. Its breeding ground was flesh, alive or dead, one reason why shepherds needed to be vigilant against it, otherwise – as I'd witnessed for myself – some of their sheep and lambs were turned into open wounds of squirming maggots!

In the case of the decomposing badger, the greenfly had thrust her oviduct (egg conducting tube) into a convenient orifice (nose, eyes, mouth, wound) and packed it tight over a period of two to three hours. This efficiently completed, she'd gone off to die, leaving her progeny to become fat maggots in two days' time, which would rapidly invade the whole carcass until it riddled and writhed like a living corpse.

I returned later the same day. The badger was almost walking, raised from the dead by an army coming to life in nature's great re-cycling process. I was awestruck! Repelled and nauseated too, but fundamentally awestruck. And watching, my mind spanned the years to my boyhood, when I'd purchased my first half-pint of maggots for fishing; walked into the shop full of rods and reels and nets and baskets, seen the man pull out a massive drawer to scoop up my order, and wondered why these less than endearing creatures were irresistible to the roach and gudgeon I hoped to catch.

The retired shepherd was adamant there were no badgers near us. The old cottager knew about a sett by the river miles away, but shared the retired shepherd's dogmatism. 'Badgers!' he said. 'Not near your place.' The farmer by whose land the dead badger was coming back to life wasn't so sure. He recalled walking through his back door to the greenhouse – admittedly three or four years ago – and disturbing a badger which brushed his leg in bolting. 'Haven't caught sound or sight of it since,' he concluded mournfully. Though, as an afterthought, he did vaguely remember a sett somewhere once in a spinney on the far side of his farm.

Just in case, I decided to check it out, but my expectations were fulfilled. Nothing. A fox earth, maybe, otherwise the place was deserted. Nevertheless the dead badger had come from somewhere, surely not all that distance away.

'Ask old Harry Gregg,' the retired shepherd advised, 'if badgers are anywhere hereabouts, he'll know. Lives at a cottage off the Great Sapling road – called Shepherd's Retreat, nice little place – you can't miss it!'

It stood back, in fact, out of sight until approached along a farm track some two hundred strides from the turn-in. I'd set out expecting to arrive within the hour. Almost two hours later I knocked on the door. No response. I knocked a bit louder. A woman appeared from round the back, accompanied by a sheepdog whose tail waved the greeting radiating from the woman's ploughed face. 'Sorry about the front door,' she said, 'we never use it. It's stuck, warped by the damp.'

She led me through a garden gate to the kitchen door, sat me down in a room obviously little used, and disappeared to find her husband. I heard loud whispers, rather like a confidence being shared with someone hard of hearing, then the shuffling of feet and finally the tapping of a stick on the stone kitchen floor. One look at Harry was enough to know he didn't move a step without effort and discomfort.

'Good morning,' he wheezed, easing himself into a chair opposite mine, requiring half-a-minute to recover. 'Badgers!' His face lit up at my enquiry. I told him of the roadside corpse. 'Exactly where?' He wanted details, more and more. 'I know the sett,' he murmured at last, 'at least I think I do; haven't been there myself for some time now.'

I mentioned the retired shepherd and the old cottager and the farmer. 'They don't appear to know about it,' I said, 'not unless it's the one the farmer had in mind, but I've already searched for that. Found nothing.'

'Not that one.' Harry smiled. 'Don't suppose it's been active for years. No, the one I mean is . . .' he started to point, then turned his piercing eyes to mine. 'Where do you say you live?' His tone suddenly changed, cautious.

Suspicious. Ten minutes or so later, presumably convinced I was truthworthy, he told me precisely where the sett could be found, but not before instructing me, making me promise, to keep the information strictly confidential. 'If you want to see them, the best time,' he advised, 'is round about dusk, not leeward, of course. If they smell your scent they'll be off like lightning.'

I promised to let him know what happened. 'Oh, something else,' he called as I left, 'a sure sign of badgers is upturned cowpats. Keep your eyes open. They turn 'em to get at the beetles.'

The reputed sett was on a bank at the edge of a wood. I found it without too much difficulty, not a cowpat in sight, on the following Saturday afternoon, hoping to check it was still in use. Harry had talked at length about badger paths and strands of badger hair – pale with dark tips – caught in barbed wire fencing; also of two or three entrances with evidence of recent digging and/or of bedding removed from the sett for airing. The other thing he'd mentioned was what he called the communal latrine, confirmation of the badger's central concern for cleanliness.

Walking gently, hardly daring to breathe, I found the entrances, one definitely indicating recent excavations, and a few strands of what I thought might well be badger's hair; but the absence of any suggestion of a latrine sowed seeds of doubt, until I came across another of Harry's tell-tale signs. The lower part of a nearby tree was heavily scratched by steel-like claws seeking freedom from mud and dirt after digging. No doubt about it, this sett was active.

Well before dusk I returned, checked the direction of the wind, and took up position, standing by a row of four trees offering cover and a near perfect view of the entrance recently worked over. It's hard to describe my feelings as I waited, apart from their ambivalence. My confidence of a sighting was somewhat constrained by a sense of it's-too-good-to-be-true, not just the sighting but my presence on such a mission – badger-watching! – at all.

In any case, the whole setting was magic, almost compensation enough whatever happened. I spotted what I thought was a fox, but couldn't investigate, terrified my slightest movement might disturb the prima donnas down below. There were, of course, plenty of sounds coming from the woods, sounds attributable in my imagination to bank- and short-tail voles, shrews and yellow-necked mice, all of which I'd recently managed to trap for a closer look before releasing, and owls and stoats successfully hunting. But primarily my mind was full of badgers, desperate my presence shouldn't be detected, warned of their acute shyness of humans.

Half-an-hour gone. By now dusk was well underway, obscuring my view of the entrance, obliterating the other two altogether. At which point I realized I'd forgotten to bring my wife's binoculars. Again. What in the world could I have been thinking about? Badger-watching without such a basic aid even in failing light! However, I did have, at Harry's prompting, a torch with a red cellophane filter, to be used, he'd emphasized, only if viewing otherwise proved impossible. Manage without it if you can, he had counselled, but if you must the badgers shouldn't mind too much; as long as, he had added, you don't make a meal of it!

Silently I stretched my legs, was thankful the dropping temperature was beginning to curtail the activity of the gnats, restricted the temptation to swot one bloating itself on my neck, and wondered for the first time how long I should hang about if nothing happened. Behind me something moved. I declined to turn round. In retrospect I accept my commitment to non-movement was perhaps excessive, but Harry had reiterated the badger's sensitive ears and sense of smell. 'If they only suspect,' he'd said, 'you'll see nothing.'

I re-checked the direction of the breeze, barely discernible. Yet again I peered at the now almost invisible entrance, tempted to switch on the torch. But suppose, the thought struck me, the switch itself makes a noise? With such an agonizing possibility nagging at my vitals I decided not to risk it. Another gnat bloated itself on my blood. Something sounded like a plop. A screech from the woods suggested a vole or mouse or rabbit had joined Nature's re-cycling operation. And then . . .

Surely that was a movement near the entrance! I strained to penetrate the darkness. A patch of white. A head.

A badger.

I couldn't believe it. Now there were two, both sniffing the air. One ventured in my direction. Nearer. Sniffing. Scratching. Suddenly the pair of them were wrestling with each other, pouncing, rolling head over heels, chasing and being chased, totally oblivious to my presence only strides away.

Still playing they moved back to the entrance, again barely discernible. Dare I use the torch? It switched on silently, and from far to my left I slowly brought the beam to focus on the gallivanters. They showed no sign of noticing, too preoccupied having fun as though explicitly for my entertainment. Sparring. Tumbling. Darting. Leaping.

One of them broke off to scratch its front paws against

a tree equidistant between the other badger and myself. Standing on its hind legs almost upright, it looked bigger than I'd supposed, demonstrating the power of its claws. Within seconds the wrestling was renewed.

A noise like shovelled gravel grew in volume, a real clatter. I moved the red beam, and watched a third badger, its bottom higher than its head, digging with its front paws, pushing the loosened soil and stones under its body to behind its hindquarters, and backing out with the load. The noise amazed me. How come such a secretive creature was so indifferent to this form of attracting attention to itself? Any 'enemy' walking in the woods could hardly have failed to hear.

This digging continued long after the other badgers had left, presumably to commence their night's hunting, and when eventually it ceased, the silence emphasized what remains for me a mystery of why this stealthy creature appears so insensitive to broadcasting its whereabouts by feverish digging. Most strange.

I lingered, I suppose, for another forty minutes or so, but was neither surprised nor too disappointed by no further sightings. What I had already seen was more than enough compensation for three hours of stoicism against the gnats!

Reminiscent of the night I saw the five foxes, I made my way home walking on air, a badger-watcher addict for life. Yet I found myself reluctant to talk to anybody but my wife about this first experience, a reaction, I've since discovered, characteristic of badger-watchers generally. I wouldn't have thought I could have felt so strongly about saying nothing, fearful undesirable ears might be listening or indirectly informed. Quite illogical, not to say unfair, of course. After all, Harry had put me wise – despite *his* initial suspicions! – and the vast majority of people shared my wish, I didn't doubt, to protect rather than harm these lovely creatures.

Even so, there was always the mindless minority – the badger-baiters whose depravity included not only incapacitating the animal before exposing it to dogs trained for killing, but dignifying this slaughter and suffering with the name of 'sport'.

Better to take no chances.

My interest in badgers acquired a new dimension after a surprising encounter in my favourite woods. Walking in the area usually worked by the craftsman pale-maker, I found his normal pitch deserted, not a sign of his tarpaulin shelter. I followed new ruts made by the tractor which collected his weekly output, and discovered him debarking and splitting poles with characteristic unhurried haste, his daily target already almost reached.

Still maintaining production, he told me of his latest spare-time enterprise, one of many – making garden furniture from odd bits of wood unsuitable for his main craft – and his gratification at the ease with which the seats and tables and wheelbarrows were snapped up. In the light of his give-away prices I understood why he couldn't keep pace with demand. Country people, in my experience, are open and fair, no more over-charging than working for charity, but here was an exception, a craftsman more in love with creating beautiful things than getting rich! I felt constrained to query whether barely covering the cost of the wood was a way to make a living? He laughed. Muttered it wasn't his real job; and told me of his latest customer, an old-age pensioner wanting a garden seat as a birthday present for her father!

'You should have seen her face when I told her how much.' His eyes danced at the remembrance.

'Did she say anything?' I asked.

'Come to think of it,' he stopped work for a moment, 'she didn't. Apart from ordering another one. I suppose that's saying enough.'

As we chatted I took in his new surroundings a clearing of coppiced trees surrounded by thick woodland, untouched by the look of things for years. No more than a dozen strides away was a pile of recently dug earth. Sheepishly he admitted he hadn't noticed it. I strolled across. A few more strides nearer the over-grown woodland was another pile, again newly dug. And a third, leading to a sizeable entrance.

'Could be badgers!' I called.

He joined me as I looked for tell-tale signs, he, a life-long woodman, excited at the prospect of seeing his very first sett. My only doubt was the nearby trees – their trunks totally free of scratches – also, as at the first sett, the apparent absence of a communal dung pit. Otherwise . . .

'I think I'll come back at dusk,' I said.

Reaching the wood while it was still quite light, I stealthily made my way through a little used area, in parts dark with overgrowth. At times, despite Hermit's Place being nowhere near, I couldn't avoid the feeling I wasn't alone; being watched. Stupid, but the impression grew. Eerie. I glanced repeatedly over my shoulder. Stood to listen. Surely footsteps. My heart raced. Through the trees came a human face.

'Hello, hello, hello,' I tried to sound unconcerned, 'what are you doing here?'

And the village policeman came fully into view. I wouldn't say he looked guilty; rather more like a man caught with his trousers down. How else to describe his embarrassment, his arrested-in-the-act air of innocence?

'People like me,' he started to explain, 'working unso-cial hours, have to take our chances whenever we can.'

And he confessed his guilty secret.

I wouldn't have suspected it. Not of our village policeman.

In extenuation I must say he tends to be unorthodox, miles removed from your average run-of-the-mill copper, perfect, in fact, for a village like ours. Which is rather like saying his prospects for promotion are less than zero. The reason is two-fold: police records for our neck of the woods suggest crime is rarely committed, let alone detected; and, second, this upholder of the law is both judge and jury, a DIY dispenser of justice on the spot. A couple of illustrations speak for themselves.

Young Joe, teenage tearabout, source of anxiety to his widowed mother, bane of his teacher's life, litter lout on the village green, sometime terrorizer of children on the swings and climbing frame, inclined to vandalism at the drop of a hat, is currently cutting the lawn every week for a couple of pensioners at the bottom end of the village, meaning not the nobs' end. Until Joe *volunteered*, the grass was like a jungle. Why this apparent change of heart? Joe had a spot of bother with the law. Nothing serious, but rather more than anti-social. He was given a thorough dressing down. And a choice. Let the law take its course or . . . a couple of pensioners needed help with their lawn.

Or take the case of Ted's car, an old banger kept on the road by faith or folly. He's a responsible young man is Ted, anxious to be law-abiding; but the price of repairs and replacements makes heavy inroads into his unskilled income. So regularly he receives a kindly tap on the shoulder, and words for his ears alone. 'This time tomor-row,' the voice says, 'I shall be back, and if that bald tyre is still on your car I'll throw the book at you.' The book hasn't been thrown yet.

I don't suppose police headquarters know too much about this, and possibly wouldn't approve if they did, but it makes for extremely effective policing. Something else, too. When politicians lament the widening gap between police and community we don't at first hand know what they're on about.

You do see, though, why – if the number of officially recorded successful cases is any criterion – our village policeman's promotion prospects are less than zero!

What, nevertheless, was he doing in my favourite wood at dusk, binoculars swinging from his neck, not a uniform or truncheon in sight, looking, to put it no stronger, a bit fraught? It did cross my mind his presence might be related to a crime in the wood shortly before Christmas. A policeman from another village, driving past, spotted a van being loaded by four unsavoury-looking characters. He stopped to ask a few questions, was hit over the head for his trouble, and came round to find the culprits long gone – a continuing cause of apoplexy for every policeman in the wider area. Yet, as much as this assault in his very own patch still especially rankled with our gentle judge-and-jury, he was, I gathered, in the wood for another reason altogether.

Seeking, would you believe, to protect a bird!

Ah, yes, but not just any old bird. He'd spotted a species virtually unknown in our part of the world, rare enough to have drawn already seven policemen from surrounding villages to take a look, all of them, as betokens ornithological fanatics, committed to maintain a warlike vigil.

'A pair of hobbies!' our guardian of the law reverently whispered, his eyes misty. 'Do you happen to know who owns this wood?' his interrogation began. 'I'd like to be sure nobody works too near the nest site.'

I promised to enquire of my woodman friend, and – wondering why I should be so surprised by our village policeman's claim to have been a keen bird-watcher for all but two of his thirty-seven years – completed my journey to the possible badger sett.

I took up my stand under the woodman's tarpaulin workshop, an ideal hide near one of the entrances, though if anything perhaps *too* near. As before I almost managed to ignore the gnats, caught up in the excitement of watching and hoping. Could it be, the thought persisted, the dead badger actually came from my favourite wood, a wood I thought I knew like the back of my hand? The question itself set my pulse racing. Yet I felt unusually calm, my mind and emotions, as it were, on ice, an attitude of stillness and patience. I mention this only because at the time it struck me as a contrast to my waiting at the other sett. Beyond doubt I was changing; just as excited, tingling with expectation, but much more a detached observer, better able, I felt, to evaluate and understand.

A pair of eyes stared in my direction. A fox. It stood for perhaps a minute, barely a movement, then tamely trotted away to the business of the night. Another fox. This time more inquisitive, doubtless ready to respond had I been free to suck on the back of my hand. I suppose I should have realized or admitted then – two quick sightings – that the *sett* was in fact an earth, confirmed by subsequent visits and sightings.

Never mind, I was learning, finding it progressively easier to be objective in interpreting the tell-tale signs, essential if I was to be sure about where badgers *didn't* live. And did. Actually, a giant step in the latter direction issued from the most devoted of the hobby-watchers. As promised I found out who owned the wood, and, passing on the information, we talked not only of birds of prey but badgers.

Did I know, our village policeman asked, about a couple of setts some half way to the *next* village?

His directions were explicit, though not, I subsequently discovered, entirely straightforward. The final turning proved self-evident, supposedly leaving me merely to cross a field, and follow a fence to the other side of a spinney, but an hour later I was still sett-less, wondering why a diagram fastidiously drawn and explained was too much for my map-reading pretensions. I retraced my steps, rummaged around, pondered how long it would take me to reach the nearest pub, and decided to take the weight off my legs as again I tried to make out where I had gone wrong. I was, need I explain, in the middle of nowhere, the only evidence of civilization a narrow track leading presumably to a farm. Once more trying to pin-point a landmark emphasized by the arm of the law, I looked up, and momentarily found it difficult to believe the undeniable.

A beautiful young woman, her swimming costume less than adequate, gliding behind a pushchair containing a child of equal loveliness. The apparition smiled, agreed it was a glorious day, and passed on. 'Excuse me,' I called, 'I'm looking for a badger sett . . .' And before I could explain further, a silky voice was telling me of an old woman in a cottage beyond the farmhouse. 'I'm staying with her,' the bikini laughed, 'come on, I'll show you the way. She'll know about badgers . . .'

I followed, the pair of us chatting about the contrast of life in the city, her normal habitat, and the country. We passed a farmhouse, more like a mansion, the home, she said, of the Hon. Mrs Climpson-Hardcastle, and continued across another field. The old cottager, gardening, heard the word *badger*, and was off to what looked like a spinney.

'It was about here,' she pointed as we arrived, 'that village children I know saw badgers only the other day; can't say I've seen any recently myself. You should ask Mrs Climpson-Hardcastle's shepherd, he's sure to know.'

I peered over the barbed-wire fence surrounding the spinney, further protected by masses of giant stinging nettles. The bikini abandoned the pushchair, skipped in the opposite direction to the old woman, and called that where she was standing looked like the best place to climb over. Eventually, grateful that not more than the legs of my trousers were caught, I fell into the spinney and stumbled over the roots of a tree buried by little more than the undergrowth. Nearby was apparently a sett entrance newly dug or enlarged by the look of things. And two more, again with suggestions of recent excavations.

Nevertheless I was sceptical. The three holes were too similar to the ones near the pale-maker's tarpaulin workshop to indicate badgers for sure. Probably another fox's earth. I moved deeper into the spinney and stopped abruptly. Surely this was the communal dung pit about which I'd heard so much but never come across before! My eyes darted. Another heap of fresh sandy soil . . . then another and another, all within near distance of a heavily scratched tree.

Badgers.

I was positive.

By the time I emerged some twenty minutes later the mother and child, like the cottager, were gone. Pity. I wanted to thank them and report *our* success. Perhaps I'd pop back to the cottage when my certainty was confirmed! Cogitating about returning to watch at dusk, wondering about getting permission from the Hon. Mrs Climpson-Hardcastle, I came across the bubbling bikini and toddler waiting for me at a cattle grid near the farmhouse. The shepherd, she pointed, lived in the cottage halfway down the hill. Furthermore the old woman wanted me to know that the farmer's wife at Magpie Farm, which I knew well, had recently reared badger cubs born after their mother's involvement in a car accident.

The shepherd's cottage was a surprise – big, almost grand, with a sizeable garden mostly of flowers. I rang the bell, determined the growling dog on the other side of the door shouldn't smell my fear. The only response was intensified barking. A tractor in an adjacent field stopped, and two men began to load logs. The older, stripped to the waist, in shorts, eyed me suspiciously, but at the mention of badgers smiled warmly.

'Lots round here,' he said, 'see 'em all the time; bloody nuisance sometimes.' And he went on to tell me of one tearing off the teats of a suckling ewe. 'Silly bugger she was,' he laughed, 'got down and couldn't get up; sheep do, you know,' he explained, 'haven't the sense to move their arse a bit to connect their feet to the ground. Kick the air like a centipede upside down. This one never did get up, more dead than alive when we found it, teats chewed right off, never seen anything like it before. No doubt a badger!'

'A badger?' I asked.

'What else?' he said.

'Well,' I began.

'Definitely a badger,' he repeated. 'Vicious little bugger. Teats gone completely. Never known it before.' The affection in his voice denied his vehemence. 'Badgers,' he continued, 'if you don't watch 'em they'll have your hand off!'

Doubtless seeing the disbelief in my eyes, he told me of catching a badger in a snare intended for a fox, and having to club it unconscious to protect himself from its steel claws as he released it. Within half-an-hour it came round, wobbled, shook itself, and soon trotted off as good as new. 'Tough little bugger.' His admiration knew no bounds.

I mentioned the suspected badger sett, and wondered whether I might keep it under surveillance? 'Anytime you like, as far as I am concerned,' he said, 'but you'd better get permission from Mrs Climpson-Hardcastle. She'll want to know what's going on. By the way,' he showed a new interest, 'what brings you to these parts? Bit off the beaten track for you, isn't it?'

I explained about the village policeman. 'If you mention his name to Mrs Climpson-Hardcastle,' the shepherd was encouraging, 'you'll be all right. He's her blue-eyed boy, can't put a foot wrong.'

So later that same day I returned to the spinney.

It was still light when I arrived, giving me, so I thought, ample time to take up position. Within two or three minutes, no more, three badgers emerged, almost catching me unconcealed. I wish I could convey my feelings, rather like watching a calf born or seeing a tropical sunset. The trio scratched like crazy, first individually and then each other, before nibbling one another's coats, to all appearances an act of special affection. After this, the larking about really started. Talk about kids let out of school! They wrestled, rolling over and over, sprang to their feet, leaped on and after each other, engaged in what for all the world looked like fisticuffs, did a lot more scratching and mutual nibbling, before beginning the furious fun and games all over again. And make no mistake. This really was *fun* not only to watch. The badgers themselves appeared to be having the time of their lives, playfully pestering each other and wanting to be pestered. The only times they stopped leaping around was for renewed nibbling, a clearly popular activity apparently no less appreciated by the nibbler than the nibbled. I can't interpret the *why* of this pleasure-giving and receiving, but it seemed, unlike the mutual scratching, to be much more than an essential part of grooming.

The larking about continued for some ten minutes, all three badgers equally involved. Then one of them disappeared into the spinney, leaving the other two to continue their game of simulated aggression. (Just like the fox cubs I once spotted playfully beating the living daylights out of each other, the vixen sprawled in the sun, picture of contented motherhood.)

From the same entrance two more badgers appeared, both much bigger, particularly one of them. They too promptly engaged in scratching and mutual nibbling of each other's hairs before the smaller introduced me to what I can only describe as the badger shuffle – rubbing its bottom along the ground as though frantically fighting off either a mammoth itch or an invasion of fleas. Meanwhile the remaining two of the first three I'd seen took themselves off, in the opposite direction to their erstwhile playmate, while the biggest badger demonstrated its size by standing upright at a tree heavily marked by claws. Doubtless the boar, it looked colossal.

By now, inclined to assume the badgers didn't mind my company, I was almost blasé in not worrying about keeping myself wholly out of sight. The badgers, despite frequently looking in my direction, appeared indifferent. Carefree. As though realizing I meant them no harm.

Only once did they seem anxious. A distant gun shot triggered the squawking of a rooks' colony on the other side of the spinney. The badgers froze and remained alert for perhaps half-a-minute before resuming their wrestling, scratching and nibbling. Otherwise they peered in my direction with total unconcern.

I now know that badgers, especially younger ones, don't see all that well. As with their foraging for food and identifying members of their own group, their defences are geared to sensitivity of hearing and above all acute sense of smell. Naturally I'd taken good care to place myself down wind. (Some badger-watchers and the like ascertain which way the wind is blowing, I've noticed, by simply holding up a wet finger; this skill eludes me. I merely dangle my handkerchief, infallible and obvious indicator.) So although the badgers spasmodically gazed in my direction, sometimes when I was unconcealed, they behaved as though I wasn't there. One came very close, as if seeking me out, but showed not the slightest alarm before disappearing presumably to search for food.

How many occupy this particular sett? Despite my frequently returning and very rarely being disappointed, I'm still not sure. Perhaps one day I shall be able to recognize each individual member of the group. At the moment it doesn't seem important. Simply to watch is pleasure enough.

14

Baa-Baa and her lamb give notice to quit

A different sort of pleasure awaited me when I returned to Shepherd's Retreat to report my badger experiences. As at my first visit, invited by Mrs Gregg to wait in the posh rather musty front room while she called her husband, I heard heavy wheezing getting nearer and nearer; then the tapping of a stick on the stone kitchen floor. Admiringly I watched as, steadied by his wife, Harry laughingly collapsed into a chair.

Still recovering some minutes later, he chipped in about his own similar badger sightings reaching back many years, clearly envious of my recent good fortune. His wife, no prompting or mention to us, brought in a pot of tea and cakes newly baked. We paid her the compliment of eating the lot, emptied the pot, and settled, the three of us, to talk about, well, this and that. A person of few words herself, she eventually invited me to follow her from the cottage through a gate at the back to an enclosure.

'This one,' she pointed, 'we've had for about fifteen years; the other about twelve.'

I surely looked what I felt.

Dumbfounded.

'It all started so unexpectedly,' she smiled, 'when I was away for a few days visiting my sister. On my return Samuel was waiting to greet me.'

'Samuel?' I said.

'Yes, he was the first. Friends of ours were schooling a couple of horses, and Samuel would insist on interfering, running after them and between them. Harry agreed to take him for a few days!'

I glanced again at one of the donkeys. 'Is this Samuel?' I asked.

'No, no,' she sounded sad, 'one of the many foals he sired over the years.'

The current pair nuzzled her for more ear kneading and nose rubbing. 'The friends schooling the horses,' she continued her story, 'decided they didn't want the donkey back. If we couldn't keep him, he'd be sent to market for auction. We kept him! What else could we do?' Her tone was answer enough.

'About a year after his coming to us,' Mrs Gregg continued, 'we entered him for a show, just for the fun of it. He was picked out for first prize, and won countless times after that. A real champion. Plenty of breeders wanted to buy him. But we don't sell pets.' She was emphatic.

Harry had joined us and his reaction suggested he wasn't entirely in agreement.

'Not *pets*,' his wife reiterated. 'Doesn't seem right somehow.' She paused. 'Instead,' she laughed, 'thinking he must be lonely, we bought him Jolly for company; and regular as clockwork they produced a foal every thirteen months. That's how long it takes for a donkey,' she shyly explained.

'I suppose Samuel's dead?' I joined in the kneading and nose rubbing.

Her face dropped. And looking wretched she made her confession:

When Samuel – note, never Sam, please – when Samuel was about sixteen, the problem of what to do with the unending foals was becoming something of a problem. Finding suitable homes – even if a giveaway donkey was wanted for the right reason – was easier said than done. Trustworthy people Harry and his wife knew or knew about didn't always have adequate accommodation!

So after much heart searching and struggling with her scruples, Harry's wife decided. Her beloved Samuel must be gelded; deprived, as she herself put it to me, 'of his bit of fun'. Within twelve months or so he was dead, attributed by the vet to a common donkey ailment – old age. She wasn't and isn't convinced. The real reason was his pining for happier days, with Jolly adding zest to life.

'He lost interest in everything,' she mourned, 'simply gave up the ghost.'

As though sharing in the lamentation, a pet goose, distinguished by the name of Fred – and I won't go into what complications this caused when my first name was revealed – waddled towards her, demanding a share of her indulgences of the donkeys. She tickled its head with a single finger, goosey ecstasy by the look of things.

'I sometimes think Fred will live forever, at least eighty,' she chuckled, 'he's twenty already.' Her eyes scanned Shepherd's Retreat's beautiful setting. 'I sit out here often,' she said, 'with the donkeys and Fred and a couple of wild rabbits that seem to have adopted us. Makes me feel so . . . contented, at peace. Isn't that so, Harry?'

'We like to walk, too,' he said, 'in those woods especially.' He nodded to a spinney barely a stone's throw beyond the donkey enclosure.

But surely he'd nearly killed himself getting from the cottage to where we were standing!

'We take our time, naturally,' he reacted to my amazement, 'no need to hurry these days . . . and we're learning, the pair of us, about things we've known all our lives. Wild flowers. Birds. Seeing isn't the same as looking! I'm changing in my old age,' he declared. 'As a young man I enjoyed shooting – rabbits, crows, that sort of thing – but not now. Even if I could.' He laughed. 'I don't want to kill anything. Nothing!' he underlined.

'Yesterday,' his wife said, 'we heard a cuckoo call 137 times, one after another without a break!'

Bubbling with her own incredulity, she disappeared to make more tea while Harry showed me his Rhode Island Red pullets, ready for market, prompting me to tell him about our anticipated battery hens. At the time they were cramped in their cages totally unaware of the continuous party to which they were shortly to be invited! But preparation for their arrival was well under way.

We'd been given – that's right, *given* – a hen house, admittedly somewhat in need of renovation. With the help of a DIY expert, whose two young children shyly asked if they could collect the eggs, we transported the gift (otherwise destined for the dump) on a trailer, precariously along the farm track to our garden gate; and were immediately confronted by a snag. Where to put it? Of course, we should have thought of this well beforehand, but the offer of the hen house came so unexpectedly, turning virtually overnight our airy-fairy plans into inescapable reality.

Until then the transformation of the battery inmates into free-range celebrants had vaguely meant their total run of the place and its surrounds. But the practical implications barely registered, crowded out by the idyll of hens wandering freely, foraging just beyond the kitchen door, producing endless eggs with maximum convenience for us and safety for them. Suddenly, collapsing hen house on a trailer at the garden gate, we glimpsed there might be more to keeping rescued battery hens than our good intentions. Like, for instance, where to put the hen house. And the more we thought about it, the man helping us waiting to unload, the more the unacceptable became unavoidable.

The paddock!

I argued this would be solving one problem only to create another. My wife countered that the paddock had never been more – or less – than an abortive ecological gesture, as much a deterrent to wild life as anything else. Finally, my head bloody but unbowed, we decided to compromise. Each of us would respect the other's point of view, and stick the hen house in the paddock.

The vandalism started. We cut back, cut down, engaged in hedging and ditching, and generally sought to make the area suitable. The hen house was repaired, creosoted, the roof insulated; and the whole heaved on to a brick foundation. All we needed now were the hens.

But we'd known for months we couldn't have them before late spring, time for the annual disposal of inmates past their best at this local battery farm. Even so, the set-up did look inviting, ideal, I had to admit, for what we had in mind. And I wasn't the only one to be impressed. Seeing the paddock's transformation, one wholly in keeping with his own priorities, the farmer with whose flock Baa-Baa was waiting to lamb wondered whether we'd like to bring our sheep nearer the cottage once she'd lambed. Casting his eyes over the paddock in relation to our kitchen window, he thought we'd enjoy having the lamb or lambs – twins? triplets? – constantly in view. 'You'll love that, I shouldn't wonder,' he indulged our eagerness.

So it was arranged. We started to count the days.

By now my wife notably was, as the jargon says, *into* lambing, revelling in it far beyond her expectations. And proving a dab hand in the process. Both before and after work, and throughout the weekends she made herself available, progressively a valued extra pair of hands for emergencies. Her interest, perhaps better described as an addiction, turned her, quite fortuitously on two separate occasions, into a life-saver.

The first was the more memorable. She was still engaged in her battle course walking to and from work, varying the route slightly during lambing to take her past the Tyler barn. The farmer, you see, had a simple system. A week or so before the first lambs were due, he housed the flock in this massive outbuilding, divided into three sections according to the planned sequence of births. The arrangement facilitated almost constant surveillance in case ewe or teg was in difficulty.

One morning as she passed she took her customary glance to check. Somehow a teg had got herself into such an awkward position that the head of her half-born lamb was already in a water trough. But such is the resilience of a healthy lamb, it was suckling within minutes, saved in the nick of time.

The second occasion was at the end of the day, as she approached the third cattle grid leading to the field adjacent to the farmyard. An invisible lamb bleating forlornly! Normally a lamb bleats to be located by its mum, usually followed by a session of suckling, but there wasn't a sheep in sight. It transpired that earlier in the day the ewes with lambs had been moved to new pasture.

Now lambs, as though you wouldn't know, are capable of getting themselves into all sorts of fixes. How many times had we disentangled a head from a fence or hedge-row! Indeed, I remember coming across a ewe of no mean strength helplessly caught in a thicket, no possibility of escape until rescued. And then there was the time we arrived too late to pull a lamb from a stream on the other side of the fence.

This invisible lamb was making one hell of a noise, out of sight yet obviously close at hand. Following the sound, my wife noticed that part of the concrete holding the cattle grid rails in position was newly chipped, allowing one of them to slip out of place; and then she spotted the lamb, three feet down, beyond doubt both frightened and hungry.

It wasn't easy to haul it to safety. But you should have seen the reunion with its frantic mum! According to my wife it was more than compensation for our much later-than-usual meal that night.

As a general rule, once the new-borns were licked clean and suckling, no time was wasted in moving them to improvised pens alongside the barn, a transfer made elementary by ensuring that the carried lambs were at the respective mother's eye level and within easy reach of her nostrils. This safeguarded, they followed their own like clockwork; otherwise rushed back to the place of birth in desperate search.

We couldn't wait for Baa-Baa's transfer. But first there was the little matter of her giving birth. Naturally we hoped to be present for the lambing itself, without seriously imagining she would be so obliging. In the event, the only thing she managed correctly was, from our standpoint, the timing.

Sunday evening. The phone rang. 'If you want to see your lamb born,' the voice said, 'you'd better get to the barn sharp.'

Within minutes we were there, gazing at a sheep showing all the usual signs of being very much in labour. She pushed. Seemed agitated. Pushed a bit more. Stood up. Lay down. Pushed again. A picture of futility.

The farmer checked, and decided to leave her a little

longer. 'We won't interfere unless we have to.' His confidence was reassuring. 'Leave her to get on with it.'

She didn't. At least, not in terms of the lamb emerging. Again he checked, soaping his hand and arm into the vagina, my wife steadying the sheep on its back and slightly lifting its backside to facilitate his deeper penetration.

'Head coming first,' he announced, apparently unconcerned.

We knew it happened frequently, simply necessitating a firm hand to push the lamb back into the womb for the front legs to be pulled forward. Perfectly straightforward. But on this occasion the lamb's left leg was proving remarkably, and inexplicably, obstinate. No trouble with the right. Presumably there was a left!

The struggle continued for perhaps ten minutes; the farmer, cool, methodical, nevertheless clearly anxious for the life of the lamb. If it wasn't born soon . . .

He unbent his back, took a breather, re-soaped his arm, and resumed the battle. Still the left leg couldn't be located. I gathered only sometime later that he'd located the leg quickly enough, but simply couldn't persuade it to co-operate. Precisely how he finally resolved the problem I shall never fully understand: his hand was lost in the sheep's innards, my wife heaved on the rear hocks, and I boldly decided not to add to the travail.

'Would you like me to phone the vet?' I sought a means of honourable withdrawal.

The last I saw he was frantically trying to get his hand deeper still, while she was seeking to lift and slightly twist Baa-Baa's hind quarters at the same time. What you might call a sobering sight for an ex-townee playing at sheep farming!

Ah, but the lamb! What a beauty. Big. Strong. Soon

searching for a teat. Quick like her mum to recover from the postponed arrival. And after the remainder of that night in the post-lambing pens, the pair were ready for transfer to the paddock.

The beginning of the end!

The first week and a half were, it's true, marvellous. Every time we left or returned to Hide 'n' Seek we were welcomed by evidence of their recognition and readiness for a session of ear kneading. Not that Baa-Baa's enthusiasm deceived us. We knew her sole motivation was food, the association of our presence with another hand-out of juicy concentrates, indisputably the joy of her life. But the lamb was something else. Gambolling. Leaping over the ditch. Springing straight up on all fours. An idyll at our own back door, guaranteed to make us feel half our age. We were enchanted.

Until we noticed Baa-Baa looking in our direction with less than her usual contentment. And the reason – once the penny dropped – was glaringly obvious. In a word, pasture. There simply wasn't enough for more than a fortnight. Apparently the farmer knew this, and acted on the assumption that our commonsense had told us likewise. It did, of course, once every blade of grass within both the paddock itself and the reach of Baa-Baa's head through the fencing was nibbled virtually down to the root.

Not to worry. Ewe and lamb were released to the farmer's lush pasture, an arrangement he was more than happy about because of my wife's frequent milking of the goats. And soon now the battery hens would surely be arriving!

This waiting period gave me an unexpected insight into intensive farming decidedly not involving hens. An eleven-year-old granddaughter with financial problems hit upon the idea of investing her meagre resources in ducks. Four. A drake and three wives. Not, need it be emphasized, as a hobby or fun pastime. This was to be strictly a business deal, an infallible means of supplementing her always inadequate pocket money.

Why ducks? For a start there was an unoccupied pond conveniently to hand; and table ducks, especially free range with their superior flavour, promised ready sales at the right price. Bound to be popular at the nobs' end of the village!

Now in a farming community like ours, you'd imagine, wouldn't you, that ducks would surely be plentiful, at least in terms of buying a quartet? But no one in the village appeared to know where *living* ducks were for sale.

I immediately perceived this was no time for undue modesty. We might be country greenhorns trying to escape our city sophistication, but in complex matters like buying breeding ducks deep in the Garden of England we knew a thing or two. Confronted by an exasperated eleven-year-old, we promptly reached for the Yellow Pages. And there it all was – name, address, phone number, a duck farm admittedly in foreign parts, a full fifteen miles away, but with an abundance of quacking inhabitants offering the widest possible choice.

The man at the duck farm told me on the phone he closed for sales on Saturdays at midday sharp. I assured him we wouldn't be late. We left in good time. Taking a wrong turning, finally hopelessly lost, we arrived with five minutes to spare. Our reception was less than wholehearted.

'Khaki or white?' the salesman pointed to two crowded pens.

The young purchaser was undone, utterly incapable of making up her mind. Once more he explained the khakis were better for eggs, the whites for eating. She was, I could see, drawn to the whites but already anxious about their logical fate!

'Five pounds, either colour.' The man looked at his watch.

'How old are they?' I played for time.

'Six weeks. Ready for the table in another fortnight. Delicious.'

'If you had a daughter of this age,' I appealed, 'wanting a drake and three ducks, what would you advise?'

His face melted. 'Follow me,' he invited.

We trailed into a building, through a second door. The child's eyes almost popped out of her head. Hundreds and hundreds of day-old ducklings, a golden mass swaying like ripe corn in a gentle breeze. The man passed more golden heads getting bigger and bigger from pen to pen. My companion, rooted to the spot, just looked. And beamed.

The man beckoned and placed in her palms a duckling of two weeks. 'Young enough,' he explained, 'to accept you as a friend, old enough not to require artificial heat.'

He handed her another and another, each struggling to jump from her grasp. She resembled a juggler, a blissfully happy incompetent juggler attempting the impossible. The ducklings leaped and squeaked. She grappled and grabbed, desperate to hang on, anxious not to hurt, almost helpless with joy. The man, now thoroughly caught up in her ecstasy, handed her another and another, filling her whole world with nothing but tiny balls of fluff. No sooner had one escaped than two more were thrust into her arms, finally overflowing, a picture of childhood rapture.

By now it was twenty-past-twelve, yet the duck farmer seemed reluctant to let us go. He chose the four for which we had come, changed his mind about one of them, explaining he wanted this special customer to have only the best, and provided a running commentary as he exercised his esoteric skill in sexing the ducklings to ensure we had no more than one drake, and no less than three ducks.

'Remember,' he offered parting advice, 'they'll be ready for the table at about eight weeks. Tasty and tender.' He smacked his lips.

We drove home in near silence, the owner of the ducklings proudly nursing the box, peeping inside, stroking a golden head soon to turn white. She also discovered, reading a pamphlet given to her by the salesman, that if she endeared herself to the quartet by regular feeding she would be able, without fear of them wandering off, to remove the enclosure already constructed round the pond.

So it proved.

There was only one drawback – initially unexpected and finally insurmountable. She loved the ducks so much she couldn't bear to think of any business transactions. 'I don't care about the money,' she declared; and added in so many words her four would be eaten over her dead body.

15

Teaching ex-battery hens to perch isn't easy

The arrival of the battery hens turned out to be as exciting and rewarding. Anticipating their coming, we chatted with neighbours, and heard such words as scrawny, scraggy, skin-and-bone, shrivelled, all warnings no less than confident assumptions, but in the event we were pleasantly surprised. I'm not claiming our lot, possibly hand-picked, were typical or likely to win a prize at our local show, but undoubtedly they looked like hens and – bearing in mind their background – generally behaved as such. Almost.

Foolishly we expected them to tear about the place in celebratory mood, immediately aware of their good fortune in having space and a new dimension of freedom; at least show some sign of pleasure, of wanting to explore the paddock and hen house. Instead they sat or stood, barely venturing, as though still imprisoned. Food alone evoked their interest; at the appearance of steaming potatoes and mash they followed my wife to the feeder and required no encouragement to help themselves. Otherwise they remained largely immobile.

Persuading them to use the hen house at all proved to be less than straightforward. Never mind that it contained sweet-smelling straw and another feeder with instant mash and a container of fresh water and plenty of perch space, they totally ignored it, preferring to squat in the soil we'd loosened for them to forage in. Even when eventually egged on to go inside – and what fun and games this produced! – they disregarded the perches completely, once more choosing to squat. Having been warned, we thought this might be the case, but nothing could have prepared us for their ineptitude in learning how to perch at all.

I placed one on, balanced it, prevented it falling off a dozen times, eased its claws round the pole, watched it sway precariously, steadied it – and picked up another to go through the same procedure. By the time number two was on, number one was off; numbers three and four on, numbers one and two off. It was rather like, I imagine, painting the Severn Bridge, the major difference being I never reached the end before finding it necessary to start all over again. An exercise in futility. These former battery hens positively refused to stay put. And no one can say we didn't try, especially on that first night. We did everything short of glueing them on. Either they didn't know, understandable enough, how to perch or they preferred not to; or perhaps a bit of both. One thing, alas, wasn't in doubt for long enough. I picked one up yet again, tried to balance it, caught it as it wobbled, felt nothing but pity, and heard an ominous sound, rather like a gurgling explosion.

My wife fell about.

I looked down, the hen still firmly in my grasp.

Take it from me, whatever their perching limitations, former battery hens remain dedicated to indiscriminate shitting, on this occasion doubtless further quickened by the nervous reaction to learning a new trick – perching. This was forgettable enough. But what of my wife's disproportionate amusement? Was it really so very funny that a vertiginous former battery hen should relieve more than its apprehension down my shirt, my trousers, my socks, and into my shoes? My wife explained it was my face!

Even so, her farmyard guffaws, causing not least the hens to squawk in alarm, sounded indecently celebratory, as though such a start to our poultry enterprise was, as she nearly choked to convey, a happy omen. She could be right. But not, I have to report, if some of our former battery farm inmates have anything to do with it. Slow they might have been at learning how to perch; but when it came to interpreting free-range as permission to fly over our garden fence they weren't slow enough.

The manual advised we cut their wings, not a word as to precisely how. I held the first wing full span. My wife snipped judiciously, every third feather. I stretched the other wing. 'I don't think we need to cut *both* wings,' she said, 'just the one; makes flight lopsided. Impossible.'

Duly impressed I reached for the next hen; and the next, each suitably trimmed on one side only, compelling subsequent flight over the garden fence with a list to port or starboard. We started again, this time less restrained with the clippers on both sides. But I mustn't give the wrong impression. Keeping former battery hens wasn't wholly chaotic.

We'd been told they wouldn't lay for days, possibly weeks, their natural reaction to such a complete change of life-style, but the very first morning an enormous egg, light brown, still warm, nestled in one of the two nest boxes. And now, months later, we rarely get less than four eggs a day from our half dozen hens; sometimes five, occasionally six. Of course, they won't lay all the year round. But the numbers aren't so important, by which I mean, although we welcome all the eggs we can get, the satisfaction of simply going to the hen house, peering into the nests, feeling the eggs one by one, and walking with them back to the kitchen never fails to confirm our confident expectations of country serendipity! The whole ritual, I can tell you – whether one egg or six, even none – tugs at something basic, perhaps primitive, in our make-up. How else to explain our profound contentment in collecting a few eggs from our own hens?

Unfortunately the hens themselves were less than satisfied, in one direction at least. First suspicions that all was not well with our cockerel was his crow, the manner in which he heralded the approaching dawn from four A.M. onwards. Initially we couldn't believe our ears. He sounded like a strangulated castrato – a series of squawks, sobs, appeals, groans, always the same four impossibly high notes repeated at least six and often a dozen times. The neighbours, hardly on the doorstep, politely inquired what was happening, and looked incredulous when we merely mentioned the cockerel.

His first recognizable cock-a-doodle-do was little short of an outrage, all effort and no achievement, rather like a hen responding to the playfulness of a fox. The noise! Again the neighbours only politely inquired. Even my wife's customary tolerance was affronted, further aggravated by the next development, an exposé of his strutting pretentiousness.

One of our hens went broody. We placed nine eggs under her, and – egged on by the grandchildren's growing excitement – began to count the days. The first week was uneventful. The hen showed not the slightest disinclination to leave the nest for feeding, otherwise didn't budge, an exemplar of devotion. The second week, however, we found it necessary to lift her off to encourage both feeding and exercise. Sounds elementary – lift her off! Yet how were we to suspect, the first time we tried, that her protectiveness of the eggs would transform her usual timidity into stabbing aggression! Subsequently we donned gardening gloves.

It was also during this second week of her sitting, as reluctantly she ate, drank, and stretched her legs, that we began to wonder and worry about something else altogether. Why did the nine eggs stink so much? Was this usual? Our poultry manual didn't mention it, any more than did our country friends. On the contrary we'd been given to understand the hen would keep the eggs no less than herself fastidiously clean throughout incubation. A bit puzzling! But undeterred, with the good intentions of the gormless, we allowed the hen to return to the nest, and assured ourselves the chicks would emerge by the end of the following week.

There was, and remains, I must say, something at times perverse about the strait-jacket of natural law. Our broody hen didn't have a chance or choice. Eggs under her wafting their stench far beyond the coop in the paddock, she remained compulsively fixed, not a doubt about ultimate success. But by the middle of the *fourth* week, we, my wife and I plus the grandchildren, were driven to conclude that a broody hen on eggs stinking to high heaven is, other considerations apart, an exercise in absolute futility.

Tenderly we lifted her off for the last time, she still frantically stabbing. Gingerly I broke one of the eggs. Just to be sure! All that remained was for me to bury to lot. Deep. The stench lingered for hours. As for the hen she responded to our indulgences, and within days was ready to return to free-range. All that awaited less straightforward attention was the cockerel's impotent gymnastics. For apart from attracting further incredulity with his castrato wailings, he paraded his aspiration to meet the requirements of egg fertilization. On a number of occasions I spotted him engaged in the essential mounted posture.

'Give him time,' the retired shepherd advised, 'he's too young to fertilize anything yet awhile; his voice hasn't even broken . . . not yet,' he laughingly added.

Maybe. But we couldn't afford such charity. Already we had a second broody hen whose compulsive sitting demanded we do everything possible to guarantee the eggs were fertile. We mentioned the problem to a neighbour.

'I've plenty,' he replied, 'how many do you want?'

The twelve he handed over, fertilized, we were assured, by cockerels of proven maturity, became the new focus of another endless vigil.

Friday night. Luby's chief mourner and his younger sister came over with their parents. Knowing all about the chicks, expected now at any moment, they fell out of the car and rushed to the paddock. 'Where are they?' Their disappointment sounded like a rebuke to more than the brooding hen. The next morning, from our bedroom window, I watched one of them creep into the paddock and peer into the coop. Suddenly he ran and in no time reappeared with his sister. He pointed. She laughed. And laughed.

My wife and I speedily joined them. A couple of golden heads were peeping from under a wing; then another and another. My wife picked one up and gave it to the little girl whose eyes were unbelieving, a picture of enchantment – bliss. Uncharacteristically her brother held his with unnerving gentleness, desperate the squeaking fluff in his cupped hands should understand his wish only to comfort. The chicks were kissed and cuddled and stroked and smoothed and assured of undying affection. All the chicks themselves wanted was, of course, to get back to the protecting wings, compelling the children to grab and juggle and spasmodically explode into merriment. I tell you, that first brood was memorable for reasons other than the successful hatching of every single one of the twelve of our neighbour's eggs.

What to do with so many? Well, for a start, former battery hens not lasting forever, we shall need a few replacements. As for the rest, we were – need I mention again – no longer sentimental about animals, certainly not all the time. Plenty of welcoming room in the deep freeze.

Meanwhile the cockerel goes on his sterile castrato way. If his voice doesn't break soon . . .

Shortly after the arrival of the chicks we were given an unwelcome demonstration of what doubtless would have happened to them but for the manual's guidance that the hen and her brood should be transferred to a protective run of their own. Incidentally, we simply carried the chicks, and, as promised in the book, the hen required no persuading to follow. Went like clockwork.

Our more immediately concern at the time was focused once more upon the dovecot. The mystery of disappearing fledglings. One after another. They were born, prospered sometimes for as long as a week, and vanished, not a sign or explanation. At first I conjectured that our symbols of peace were again directing their viciousness inexplicably against their own. My only doubt was the absence of corpses, but, remembering the four or five I'd discovered buried deep when cleaning out the dovecot months before, I didn't seriously seek another explanation. Indeed, I was resigned to believing that Mother Nature knew best.

We welcomed another pair of dove fledglings, saw their pink nakedness beginning to turn featherly white, and assumed their total acceptability. The next time I looked they were gone. To be honest, I seriously wondered whether I'd been seeing things. Perhaps I'd imagined the fledglings, mistaking them for the constant to-ing and fro-ing of the other doves. How else to explain another conspicuously empty nest?

Then one morning, wakened by a particularly noisy dawn chorus, I made for the paddock to feed the hens. The doves were cooing on the cottage roof, unusually agitated, compelling my attention. I glanced at the dove-cot. At the foot and widely scattered were innumerable white feathers, evidence of a kill. Leo? That magnificent monster again! Wishing upon him his just deserts, I fumingly opened the paddock gate, and, barely able to believe my eyes, froze on the spot.

The half de-feathered dove on the ground, unmistakably still alive, made no attempt to move. Its exposed flesh, a bloody oozing mess, was already receiving the frenzied attention of a giant bluebottle, quick to exploit this perfect opportunity to multiply itself. As with the 'corpse' of the bird from the chimney, I found myself momentarily overwhelmed by a mixture of awe, pity and anger; awe because of this encounter with the terminal, pity and anger because such suffering was an outrage.

What to do? The dove must be put out of its misery, no question, yet for me the distance between this obligation and its fulfilment seemed as wide as the world. Unbridgeable. Screwing myself up, I grabbed a spade and aimed with excessive strength to guarantee an instanteous dispatch. Then, ignoring my avowed commitment to Nature's great re-cycling process, never more sure, in fact, that on this occasion ritualistic reverence of some sort was essential, I dug a hole and silently performed the last rites.

All that now remained was to work out what had happened. But there wasn't time to think. An unholy cacophony swung my eyes to the dovecot, and out popped a couple of magpies, one with an egg in its beak, the pair doubtless disappointed the booty wasn't another fledgling! No wonder the countrymen and women I know detest the bird, and jump at every opportunity for decisive action. Not that I, you understand, with my literal views, feel any antagonism towards the magpie – or a similar marauder the crow – as a species. After all, no one can blame the murderous brutes for being themselves, fulfilling their own natural urges, occupying the role for which presumably if inexplicably they were intended. I simply draw the line when it comes to our doves being savaged as they try to defend their own. And whenever my intolerance is tempted to weaken, I have a vision of a near de-feathered dove, its flesh stabbed open by a pneumatic drill camouflaged as a magpie's beak. More than enough to sustain the state of war between us!

Virtually every other species of bird evokes the opposite reaction. We derive endless pleasure watching swallows, for instance, playing in and around the cottage of our nearly ninety-year-old neighbour and his wife, both knowledgeable observers of the natural world, and certain that the same birds return year after year. I heard on the radio, experts insist that swallows don't necessarily return to their old nests. Respectfully our neighbours disagree; they know their birds at sight, and watch for their arrival, a reunion of old friends. The swallows in residence at the moment, they informed us the other day, arrived a clear eight days before the first sound of the cuckoo, unique in their long involvement with both species.

What convinces the old couple they're right about their particular swallows is that the nest to which they return is, following an extension to the porch, virtually inside the cottage, hardly a likely choice without a bit of inbred knowledge.

It's straightforward enough to understand why the height at which swallows fly is believed to be a reliable predictor of the weather. Insects, their staple diet, fly higher in the sun, lower as the temperature drops.

Less easy to appreciate is why traditionally in the country swallows are welcome as good omens. To have them nest on your property is a sign of coming prosperity. If, however, they desert the nest the outlook is threatening.

I take all this with a pinch of salt, but watching these majestic little birds in flight I'm not at all surprised to learn that the imagined beneficial effects of their closeness to people's homes is – or perhaps more correctly was – believed to extend to recipes for healing. Swallow broth was thought to be a remedy for both epilepsy and stammering, though how such faith was sustained without presumably the right results must remain another mystery. Whatever the reason, my wife and I continue to enjoy their incredible aerial movements, and marvel that their seemingly delicate bodies don't fall apart.

She – ornithologically miles ahead of me – found herself cultivating a relationship with a blackbird – or was it the other way round? Bold as brass, hardly hesitating, it hopped on to the step of our kitchen door, as though invited to breakfast.

My wife threw a few crumbs, then some more, a few landing on the doormat. Hardly hesitating it hopped forward and ate the lot. At lunch time it was back for more. The daily visits continued for about a week, the bird as venturesome as a mouse on the bird table. Having itself first eaten a little, it loaded its beak and flew off, repeating the exercise time after time.

Then days later, two fledglings accompanied the parent bird to the source of supply. Initially they kept their distance, squawking, protesting, appealing, looking indignant if not incensed at their feeder's apparent refusal to be hurried. Yet time after time she stuffed her beak, hopped to the middle of the patch of grass we call our lawn, and rammed the food down their throats. Within seconds they were screaming for more.

Fascinating to watch; but I kept worrying. Warning. The mother bird would come to rely upon our charity, so what happens when we're away? And the fledglings, wouldn't they lack the ability adequately to fend for themselves? This apart, with such feastings in the middle of our green patch, what about the prowling felines? In our bit of the country they – countless ferals plus Leo – knocked off one bird after another. This no longer offended me, as I've tried to indicate; after all, cats will be cats. But this didn't grant us the right to give already vulnerable birds a false sense of security with easy pickings from our doormat and lawn!

My wife quietly suggested I was underestimating the intelligence of both the birds and herself!

My fears, I have to admit, proved groundless. The fledglings continued to emulate their mother's audacity, all three of them arriving at the back door as though by appointment to demand the handouts to which they'd become entirely accustomed. And in the fullness of time, the trusting trio, long independent of doormat charity, transferred their patronage to the bird table.

Blackbirds generally, we've noticed, are either remarkably tame or lacking in appropriate caution. Other birds, with the notable exceptions of thrushes, sometimes chaffinches, and of course robins, act on the assumption humans can't be trusted. Their instinct is to stay wary,

216

rather like the chirpy house sparrow which appears friendly enough without for a moment dropping its guard. The four species I've mentioned, though also naturally wary, seem, on the other hand, to have built into their fundamental make-up a spontaneity of trust of humans. I wonder why.

16

The other side to living in the country

An animal unfortunately not of this trustful number, for
reasons of the sometimes insane cruelty of its only predator – man! – was rapidly becoming, as you might have
guessed by now, my favourite: the badger.

Unknown to almost the entire village, our neighbourhood was teeming with the lovely creatures! One in
particular, for this very reason, continued to haunt me –
the badger brought back to life, not the macabre nature
of its resuscitation, but the place of its roadside death
relative to the nearest sett I knew.

Badgers, as I've already mentioned, rarely travel far
from their home base. This one was more than a mile as
the crow flies. Surely there was another sett nearer the
scene of the accident! The fact remained, I'd searched
high and low; and as knowledgeable villagers kept telling
me, we didn't have badgers in our immediate area. Their
confidence didn't surprise me. After all, we ourselves had
been hereabouts for long enough before stumbling across
the contrary evidence. Until then, neither sight nor scent
of a badger.

Nevertheless, I couldn't or didn't stop looking, poking
around in my favourite wood, earths aplenty, not a sign
of a badger. My woodman friend, frequently moving his
tarpaulin workshop, introduced me to parts of the wood
I'd never systematically searched before, all to no avail.
If the dead badger had come from the nearer sett, it
certainly wasn't in our direction!

He, the pale-maker, was still keen to set eyes on his

first badger, but his much greater interest – apparently unrelated to my search – were boot fairs, proliferating in our wider neighbourhood, an easy means, he was finding, of supplementing his regular income. Folk will buy anything, he smiled, any bit of old rubbish on offer. If only he could persuade more people to clear out their attics, or farmers to sell him the bits and pieces left to rust or rot in barely standing barns and outbuildings. He'd make a fortune! The theme brought up his search of the ruins of a farm labourer's cottage no more than half-a-mile from where we were talking. I'd heard about it before, actually spoken to a villager who claimed his father had been brought up there, but never managed to find it or any trace. What intrigued me was not possible booty for a boot fair, but the reputed isolation of the place, by comparison turning our lonely setting into a built-up area. I resolved to try again.

The woodman's careful instructions confirmed I'd been looking in approximately the right place, and this time I found it, a pile of rubble unrecognizable as a former cottage. I sat for, I suppose, about half-an-hour, awed by the thought that the eerie silence had once echoed with the whole gamut of human emotions; and not altogether sure all the former residents had taken their final leave! The place seemed haunted.

I climbed, or rather avoided some wire-netting fencing, followed the hedge of a field of ripe wheat, and – if not saddened then subdued – completed the walk home in about ten minutes.

Later that same night I drove to the badger sett I'd first learned about from Harry.

'Pity it's so far away.' I told my wife about the fun and games I'd again hugely enjoyed.

'You ought to be only too pleased . . .' she said.

I was.

But that dead badger wouldn't lie down. Somewhere near or nearer there had to be another sett. Surely. Yet there wasn't. I'd searched everywhere; everywhere, in fact, apart from – the realization honestly hit me like a shaft of light – the surrounds of the old cottage!

'Don't be so sure,' my wife counselled caution as I prepared to return; but I felt in my bones this was it! There *was* nowhere else, not near us. And when eventually I found three entrances with signs of recent excavations, then more entrances, indicators of a sizeable group, my previous certitude in no way detracted from the excitement of confirmation. Only badger addicts, I imagine, will understand.

The next step was, of course, actually to see the badgers. Two nights later, my first opportunity, I retraced the short distance across a field, a lane, three more fields, and there in sight were the trees marking the spot. I stood for a moment in disillusionment if not disbelief. Two combine harvesters and two tractors with trailers were gathering in the wheat, one of the latter within a dozen strides of the sett on the other side of the hedge. The driver, whom I knew well, spotted me in the distance and waved. I waved back, inwardly fuming that he and his men were there at all at such an hour! Never mind that he owned the field and surrounding land, including my hoped-for badger sett.

Surreptitiously, not wishing my purpose to be suspected, I slipped into the trees on the far side and made my way to where I planned to watch, not doubting for a moment that if the harvesting continued much longer my mission was hopeless. Whenever the machines were close I crouched lower to avoid detection, eventually took up my position, and almost immediately changed it. The lower branches of a tree closely overlooking the entrance under surveillance offered a grandstand view, always supposing the farmer and his fellow labourers did the decent thing and cleared off. As dusk closed in, they switched on the headlights.

The thought occurred I might as well go. In truth, I would have gone but for wondering how to explain my sudden emergence at such an hour. I didn't want anyone to know I suspected the presence of badgers, yet what else could I say if challenged?

I stayed.

And as the machines still thundered to and fro, the first badger emerged to sniff the air. I nearly laughed out loud. It looked so outraged, like a maiden aunt tracing a bad smell; and having filled its lungs with diesel fumes and the scent of humans it disappeared below. A sighting of no more than ten seconds, if that, but in my excitement I almost fell out of the tree. For now I knew for sure. This was the sett from which the killed badger had come, no more than half-a-mile from the scene of the accident. And not another living soul, as far as I knew, certainly nobody in the village, had the slightest idea.

My very own badger sett!

For all that, living in the country, honesty compels me to concede, isn't necessarily all gain. Not quite. Not all the time. The mud gets no thinner, the shops no nearer, humping the weekly dustbin bag to the end of the farm track over the horizon no easier, keeping the cesspit co-operative no simpler; our village doctor is second to none, but the nearest hospital is ten miles away, hardly handy for emergencies. In any case, adverse weather is liable, as recently, to cut us off completely, a wonderful inducement to community spirit but otherwise less appealing,

221

especially with my wife stranded in the next village!

Nevertheless – and about this the pair of us are absolutely agreed – a mammoth consolation remains. Forget our fun and games with sheep and lambs and goats and doves and battery hens and foxes and even my beloved badgers, this one thing transcends the lot.

We noticed it soon after arriving here, not entirely convinced. Even in those balmy days it seemed just a little too good to be true. Simply incredible! But as the weeks and months and years slipped by, it couldn't be doubted. And now the longer we stay the more convincing it becomes. On *our* side of the fence, too: *the grass is greener*.